The Nurse's Reality Gap

Overcoming Barriers Between Academic Achievement and Clinical Success

Leslie Neal-Boylan,
PhD, CRRN, APRN-BC, FNP

Sigma Theta Tau International
Honor Society of Nursing®

Sigma Theta Tau International
Honor Society of Nursing®

The Honor Society of Nursing, Sigma Theta Tau International (STTI) is a nonprofit organization whose mission is to support the learning, knowledge and professional development of nurses committed to making a difference in health worldwide. Founded in 1922, STTI has more than 130,000 active members in more than 85 countries. Members include practicing nurses, instructors, researchers, policymakers, entrepreneurs and others. STTI's 486 chapters are located at 662 institutions of higher education throughout Australia, Botswana, Brazil, Canada, Colombia, England, Ghana, Hong Kong, Japan, Kenya, Malawi, Mexico, the Netherlands, Pakistan, Singapore, South Africa, South Korea, Swaziland, Sweden, Taiwan, Tanzania, the United States, and Wales. More information about STTI can be found online at www.nursingsociety.org.

Sigma Theta Tau International
550 West North Street
Indianapolis, IN, USA 46202

To order additional books, buy in bulk, or order for corporate use, contact Nursing Knowledge International at 888.NKI.4YOU (888.654.4968/US and Canada) or +1.317.634.8171 (outside US and Canada).

To request a review copy for course adoption, e-mail solutions@nursingknowledge.org or call 888.NKI.4YOU (888.654.4968/US and Canada) or +1.317.634.8171 (outside US and Canada).

To request author information, or for speaker or other media requests, contact Rachael McLaughlin of the Honor Society of Nursing, Sigma Theta Tau International at 888.634.7575 (US and Canada) or +1.317.634.8171 (outside US and Canada).

ISBN: 9781937554460
EPUB ISBN: 9781937554477
PDF ISBN: 9781937554484
MOBI ISBN: 9781937554491

Library of Congress Cataloging-in-Publication Data

Neal-Boylan, Leslie.
 The nurse's reality gap : overcoming barriers between academic achievement and clinical success / Leslie Neal-Boylan.
  p. ; cm.
 ISBN 978-1-937554-46-0 (book : alk. paper) -- ISBN 978-1-937554-47-7 (ePUB) -- ISBN 978-1- 937554-48-4 (pdf) -- ISBN 978-1-937554-49-1 (mobi)
 I. Sigma Theta Tau International. II. Title.
 [DNLM: 1. Nurse's Role. 2. Clinical Competence. 3. Education, Nursing. 4. Job Satisfaction. 5. Nurses--supply & distribution. 6. Personnel Management. WY 87]

 610.73--dc23
                                        2012047799

First Printing, 2013

Publisher: Renee Wilmeth
Acquisitions Editor: Emily Hatch
Editorial Coordinator: Paula Jeffers
Cover Designer: Michael Tanamachi
Interior Design/Page Layout: Katy Bodenmiller

Principal Book Editor: Carla Hall
Content & Project Editor: Kate Shoup
Assistant Editor: Jennifer Lynn
Proofreader: Barbara Bennett
Indexer: Jane Palmer

Dedication

To my dad, Edward Rotkoff (the "blond tiger"), and my children, Paul, Cori, Andy, and Bonnie, with lots of love.

Acknowledgments

I would like to thank all of the nurses who responded to the survey and shared their insights and experiences for the purposes of this book. It has been a pleasure and an honor to work with the excellent editorial staff at Sigma Theta Tau International. I would also like to thank Claryn Spies for her generous assistance with this project.

About the Author

Leslie Neal-Boylan, PhD, CRRN, APRN-BC, FNP

Leslie Neal-Boylan is associate dean and professor at Quinnipiac University in Hamden, Connecticut. She earned her BSN from Rutgers University, her MSN from San Jose State University, and her PhD in nursing from George Mason University. She received a postmaster's certificate as a family nurse practitioner (FNP) from Marymount University. She is a board-certified family nurse practitioner and is certified in rehabilitation nursing, home health nursing, and rheumatology. She maintains a clinical practice as an FNP. Neal-Boylan has more than 30 years of direct clinical experience and 15 years in nursing education. She has held various leadership positions in nursing throughout the years. She has authored and/or edited almost 100 peer-reviewed publications, including seven books. Neal-Boylan's research focus has been on the nursing workforce, most recently concerning registered nurses with disabilities and retired volunteer nurses. However, she has also published on topics related to geriatric patient care, the nurse practitioner role, and chronic illness.

Table of Contents

Preface

When I first set out to write this book, my objective was to discover how it felt to be newly graduated as a registered nurse. This book was originally envisioned as a way to share the experiences of nurses transitioning from student to professional. My hope was that new graduates could read about the experiences of their peers and perhaps circumvent the difficulties that had arisen for their predecessors. I knew that nursing had changed in many ways since I graduated in 1981; some changes were clearly for the better, but other changes concerned me. I knew anecdotally and from articles and professional conversations that many nurses, especially recently graduated nurses, were and are leaving nursing. I come from a long line of nurses, and I love being a nurse, so I despair that there will be fewer enthusiastic nurses to take my place when I become too old to do what I love.

I did not intend to conduct a formal research study. I just wanted to get a general sense of how recently graduated nurses felt about being nurses. I also realized that very little had been done to explore the experiences of nurses who recently completed graduate degrees. I determined that an online survey could be the perfect vehicle for obtaining this information. To gather this information, an assistant and I sent announcements and the link to the online survey to 180 nursing schools and 50 student nurse associations. We also distributed the announcement at nursing conferences. The assistant helped me to collate and organize the responses.

The original idea was to obtain responses from graduates of diploma, associate, baccalaureate, master's, and doctoral degree programs. We received slightly fewer than 100 responses—none from diploma graduates and only a few from doctoral graduates. The rest were approximately evenly divided.

Any good researcher would cast doubt on the validity of information gleaned from 100 responses, especially when those responses are divided into three groups. Keep in mind, however, that most responses from associate-degree graduates are very consistent with those of baccalaureate-degree graduates. In addition, master's-prepared graduates have heretofore been an underrepresented group with regard to new graduate experiences. If I had it to do over again, I would design a formal research study—something I still think is worth pursuing, especially in light of the interesting responses I received.

I realized as I read through the responses that not only would they be helpful for nursing students and other new graduates, but they would also inform nurse educators and leaders about how recent graduates feel about nursing and their preparation to enter the profession. The book morphed into a discussion about what is right and wrong in nursing and what we might need to fix as we move into the future.

There is no substitute for formal and rigorous research methods to gather sufficient high-quality data from which to draw reliable and valid conclusions. However, the responses gleaned from this more casual survey are valuable nonetheless, because they provide a window into how new graduates feel. Moreover, their experiences confirm much of what is already in the literature. One might fairly say that only people with complaints respond to informal surveys. It is interesting to note, though, that many positive comments came through from the survey, and the responses give us many reasons to be proud of our profession and of our graduates.

I would also like to say a word about the integration of my own perceptions in the book. After being in nursing for more than 30 years in a variety of professional settings and positions, I feel that I have earned the right to reflect on my own observations about nursing and to comment on what I think we do well and what we could do better. Some readers will find similarities between my perceptions and their own. Others may think me harsh and that my thoughts don't apply to them or their experiences in nursing. In that case, I'd be relieved that my experiences may not be as pervasive as I think. I encourage nurses, regardless of their perspectives, to open up or continue a dialogue about what is working and what is not. Clearly, the exodus of nurses can only be interpreted as catastrophic to the profession. Let's work together to strengthen what is working and to fix what is not.

–Leslie Neal-Boylan

Foreword

In *The Nurse's Reality Gap: Overcoming Barriers Between Academic Achievement and Clinical Success*, Leslie Neal-Boylan presents a thorough assessment of the work of new nurses and gets at the crux of the issues of retention and burnout: the meaningfulness of nurses' work lives. While there is much in the literature identifying specific factors leading to burnout and retention issues, including research and expert opinions, Neal-Boylan approaches the topic by going directly to nurses for their thoughts, experiences, and opinions. She also offers very specific tips for new nurses, summarizing lessons learned from the field. *Every new nurse should carry these tips with them on a smartphone or a note card.* The advice is easy to take for granted but also easy to forget when nurses are caught up in day-to-day work. Mentorship, for example, is critical, as are asking questions and networking with other nurses to ease the transition from the academic world to clinical work.

A unique and important feature of this book is the inclusion of content about newly prepared graduate-level nurses, including those with doctorates. An often-overlooked group, these nurses also face challenges transitioning into new roles, and some of the same strategies can be useful for brand-new nurses and those making major professional changes. I have personally had the advantage of having the same professional mentor throughout my career, a nurse in whom I have the utmost trust. I value her opinion on any issue and have sought her advice routinely. Before the time of instant communication, I knew that I could make a collect call to her from anywhere in the world. Every nurse should have a mentor who will be available for advice, support, coaching, and care. This message is communicated loud and clear in the voices of the nurses throughout this book.

There are many important lessons in the words of the nurses represented here. Nurse educators and nurse leaders in health care facilities are reminded of the need to build and implement support structures to smooth the transition to new roles. We know that mentorship and fellowship programs matter, yet not all health care facilities offer these programs. The added value far outweighs the program costs, particularly when considering the costs of nurse replacement, which are approximately twice the annual salary of the nurse. For preparation of nurses at the graduate level, there is an identified need for both education and management courses. Our health care and educational institutions would be well served if nurses prepared at the graduate level had these skills. It is also heartening to note that graduates of these advanced-degree programs identified a need for more research and publication skills. The profession will indeed be better served if we enhance our graduate education and stretch students beyond their comfort zone.

This book is timely, given the recommendations of the 2010 Institute of Medicine (IOM) *Future of Nursing* report. Noteworthy is the refrain of some of the associate degree-prepared nurses that they should have opted for the baccalaureate degree in the beginning. Other messages from nurses are also consistent with the IOM report, including the need for more residency programs and the need to focus on primary and community care, as demands for acute care are changing.

Without a doubt, the most important contribution of this book is in capturing the many questions that abound within the nursing profession. Neal-Boylan raises issues that often have remained dormant in our intellectual and professional discussions. These issues are important if we are to restructure our educational and practice programs. More importantly, many of these unresolved issues lead to the professional chasms identified by Neal-Boylan. The discussion and debate will be enhanced through this frank acknowledgement that resolving professional differences may well be a wise investment in future nursing generations.

–Joyce J. Fitzpatrick, PhD, MBA, RN, FAAN

Introduction

The fact is, new nurses are leaving the field of nursing at an alarming rate (Black, Spetz, & Harrington, 2008, 2010; Wood, 2013). With fewer nurses, there is a tendency to employ unlicensed personnel and people who are not as well-educated as RNs to care for patients. The use of unlicensed personnel, especially, has resulted in fatalities and patient complications that should not have occurred. Technically, there really is no shortage of nurses today. There are 3 million nurses in this country. However, there is a shortage of nursing jobs, because organizations do not seem to grasp that "you get what you pay for." That is, it is worthwhile paying to employ RNs rather than less-educated health care workers, because RNs improve the quality of patient care, and their work leads to better patient outcomes. With the ebb and flow of nursing shortages in the United States, doing everything possible to retain nurses is imperative. To do this, one must first grasp why nurses leave.

Nurse Retention and the Meaning of Nursing

Recent years have seen tremendous focus on the issues of nurse retention and satisfaction. Researchers have identified a variety of factors that influence nurses' decisions whether to remain in their jobs and in nursing. According to a 2009 study by Morgan and Lynn, much of what provided satisfaction to nurses had to do with the *meaning* of nursing—in other words, providing comfort to patients, interacting with them, and advocating for them.

The researchers found that nurses in the study felt that the nursing shortage had to do with not having enough help from nurses who were skilled and experienced enough to address the needs of patients. Participants in this study put much of the blame on inadequate training or orientation of new nurses.

NOTE

According to the Morgan and Lynn (2009) study, other keys to job satisfaction for nurses are the interactions nurses have with each other and with their patients. Receiving support from coworkers was particularly significant. However, many nurses noted that a lack of resources—mostly with regard to staff—required them to work harder to do the work that was necessary. Researchers concluded that in addition to extrinsic rewards such as pay, it is important for nurses to experience intrinsic satisfaction through their relationships with coworkers, patients, and other nurses. Nurses also valued the autonomy they gained as they became more experienced and enjoyed mentoring less-experienced nurses. (Researchers described "autonomy" as having control over one's work and being able to prioritize work without being closely supervised.)

Preparing Nurses for the Clinical Setting

The literature abounds with the need to better prepare registered nurses to practice in a clinical setting. Nursing schools are continually pressured to add more content to best train new graduates to begin in their roles as nurses (Ulrich et al., 2010). Another study—this one focusing on new nurses and their transition into the profession, conducted in 2009 by the National Council of State Boards of Nursing—demonstrated that even after 2 and 3 years of practice, nurses still do not feel entirely comfortable and confident about making clinical decisions, planning and initiating care, and communicating with physicians (Hoffart, Waddell, & Young, 2011).

Pertaining to these issues, a 2010 report by the Institute of Medicine, *The Future of Nursing*, has established several recommendations:

- Nurses should practice to the full extent of their education and training.

- Nurses should achieve higher levels of education and training through an improved education system that promotes seamless academic progression.

- Nurses should be full partners with physicians and other health care professionals in redesigning health care in the United States.

- Effective workforce planning and policymaking require better data collection and an improved information infrastructure.

Improving Nursing Education

On the topic of receiving higher levels of education and training through an improved education system, the Carnegie study (Benner, Sutphen, Leonard, & Day, 2010) advocates for the following:

- Nursing must undergo major changes to prepare new nurse graduates for practicing in the profession.

- There must be significant increases in the number of students admitted to nursing schools to meet the demand for nurses both now and in the future.

- Entry-level positions in nursing should require a baccalaureate degree.

- Baccalaureate-prepared nurses should be encouraged to pursue graduate degrees, partly to increase the number of nursing faculty. (Some nurse leaders support the continuation of associate-degree programs but note that their graduates should be strongly encouraged to pursue the baccalaureate degree.)

- Clinical courses should be integrated into the curriculum in the first 2 years of the baccalaureate program. This will both introduce students to nursing and prepare them for the reality of community-based nursing by offering more clinical experiences in settings other than in acute care.

> **NOTE**
>
> *The Robert Wood Johnson Quality Safety Education for Nurses (QSEN) initiative offers resources to help promote excellence in new nurse graduates, both clinically and in health care (http://blog.rwjf.org/humancapital/category/nursing/). Suggestions are available through QSEN for nurse educators of both undergraduate and graduate students to help educators teach in ways that promote excellence.*

Improving the Workplace

Of course, education is not the only area that needs work, as evidenced by a qualitative study of nurses in their first year practicing in the hospital setting (Martin & Wilson, 2011)—a year that has been described by many authors and researchers as the most difficult in the career of a nurse (Blanzola, Lindeman, & King, 2004; Casey, Fink, Krugman, & Probst, 2004). Researchers in the Martin and Wilson study were particularly interested in two themes that appear in the literature: the acculturation of the professional (Kramer, 1974) and the responsibilities of the professional (Benner, 1984).

The Acculturation of the Professional

In her 1974 book *Reality Shock: Why Nurses Leave Nursing*, Marlene Kramer discussed the discrepancy between the education the student received and actual nursing practice. Kramer described the inherent phases of acculturation as being the honeymoon phase, the shock and rejection phase, the recovery phase, and the resolution phase. Initially, the new nurse is excited and enthusiastic about finishing his or her degree and beginning in the profession (honeymoon). Following this phase, the nurse becomes disillusioned (shock and rejection). With experience, the nurse gains perspective and begins to recover (recovery). Finally, the new nurse must decide how to move forward—whether to adapt to or leave the current position or go back to school (resolution).

> **NOTE**
>
> *Relationships appear to be significant to the ability to adapt—particularly relationships with physicians and other staff. In addition, relationships with other nurses seem integral to a good experience as a new graduate (Kramer, 1974; Martin & Wilson, 2011).*

Hoffart, Waddell, and Young (2011) also write about reality shock and how it continues to hamper transitions for new nurses. They acknowledge Kramer's assertion that it is vital for new graduate nurses to move beyond feelings of shock and find ways of overcoming their disillusionment and anger.

Nursing schools have found various ways to better prepare new graduates for this difficult transition. Among these is clinical experience that is precepted during the final year of school. In general, students who have had preceptors seem to feel more comfortable with the expectations of the nursing role (Wieland, Altmiller, Dorr, & Wolf, 2007). Other programs that have been studied include externships, cooperative education programs, and nurse residencies. (Of course, it is difficult to determine how formal programs to aid new nurse transition affect new nurses in the long term [Hoffart et al., 2011].)

The Responsibilities of the Professional

In her 1984 book *From Novice to Expert: Excellence and Power in Clinical Nursing Practice*, Patricia Benner wrote about the experience of being a novice nurse and how nurses progress through several stages to become expert nurses. The novice nurse struggles with the basics of nursing practice. As the nurse gains experience and competence, he or she gains perspective on what it means to be a nurse and how to perform well.

According to Martin and Wilson (2011), managers, preceptors, and educators are responsible for nurturing new nurses as they move through the phases of development. They advocate for instructing staff in what to realistically expect from the new graduate. Opportunities to safely debrief during the first year can help new nurses with their transition. They also differentiate between preceptors who care about the nurses they precept and preceptors who do not—and how this can strongly affect the development of the new graduate.

About This Book

In an effort to address the issues touched on in this introduction, this book presents the voices of actual nurses sharing their experiences as new nurses. This book is not based on a research study. However, an online survey tool elicited responses (please read the preface for more information pertaining to the survey method). Nursing schools throughout the country as well as nursing associations and a variety of media advertised the survey.

Survey responses highlighted many important themes about the experience of being a new nurse that are reflected in the current literature.

For example:

- Nurses with associate degrees who responded to the survey conducted for this book largely acknowledged that they needed a baccalaureate degree and, in some cases, wished that they had gone to school for a baccalaureate degree instead of an associate degree.

- Nurses who responded to the survey frequently addressed the need for increased and more realistic clinical experiences and assignments while in school.

- Several nurses noted that they wished they had had more experience in community-based settings while still in school.

- New nurses acknowledged the need to further their education.

- Many new nurses recognized the importance of health care reform and the need for nursing to play a large role in reform.

- Many nurses who responded to the survey remarked that the longer they were in nursing, the more they could appreciate what it meant to be a nurse. Many lamented that they did not learn this in school because of the emphasis on skills and the nitty-gritty of learning how to be a nurse. New graduates seemed to value nursing more after they had learned to prioritize and manage their time and had mastered the basic functions of the job; it was at that point that they could begin to simply comfort patients.

NOTE

In her book Transforming Presence: The Difference That Nursing Makes *(2008), Margaret Newman, a noted theorist, highlights that transformative learning (Watson-Gegeo, 2005) can "help students become who they will become rather than be 'trained'" (Newman, 2008, p. 75). Newman and transformative learning advocate that students experience "the deep interpersonal relationship with another" (p. 76).*

- Having a mentor appeared to be the most important factor in making a good adjustment as a new nurse.

- Many new nurses described initially feeling intimidated by doctors, but realizing "they are people, too" helped them adjust to these interactions.

However, the literature is scarce with regard to the experience of those recently graduated from a master's or doctoral program. Hopefully, this book can shed more light on the experience of being a new graduate nurse and draw more attention to the experiences of nurses whose roles have changed due to graduate education.

Many books provide tips to new nurses about what to do as they begin their jobs, but this book describes how new nurses see the profession and what they believe can help new graduates make the transition to nursing professionals. In addition, the perspectives of nurses who recently earned graduate degrees add something new to the literature. This book is by no means the final word on the subject of the experiences of new nurses. Rather, it should stimulate discussion, debate, and research to explore these phenomena further. Hopefully, this book will give food for thought on how recent graduates view their education and themselves. Their thoughtful responses and advice can help students who are about to graduate and recently graduated nurses see they are not alone in their transition. In addition, nurse educators would be wise to heed the suggestions the respondents offer for improving nursing education, so that future new graduates feel better prepared to join our proud ranks.

Chapter 1
The Associate Degree-Prepared Nurse

It is estimated that about 50% of nurses in the United States (US) have an ADN or diploma in nursing (Health Resources and Services Administration [HRSA], 2008). The associate-degree is typically acquired after a 3-year program of study (American Association of Colleges of Nursing [AACN], 2011). Graduates from associate degree programs are eligible to sit for the board exam to become registered nurses. But what is it like to be a recently graduated nurse with an associate degree in nursing (ADN)? Do ADN graduates feel prepared for their roles as novice nurses? Do they see a need to go on to receive a baccalaureate degree in nursing (BSN)?

Because there has been increasing emphasis on the baccalaureate degree for entry into nursing practice—indeed, according to the AACN, RNs with BSNs have risen in number and those with associate degrees as their highest degree have declined, and nurses with associate degrees and diplomas are earning baccalaureate degrees in increasing numbers (as cited in AACN, 2011)—it is interesting to explore how graduates of associate-degree programs in nursing perceive their preparation to enter the nursing workforce and how they view the quality of their work experiences.

According to the National Advisory Council on Nurse Education and Practice, a minimum of two-thirds of the workforce in nursing should have at least a BSN (as cited in AACN, 2011). And the Institute of

Medicine (IOM) notes that those with ADNs and diplomas should begin baccalaureate degrees within 5 years of graduation (2010).

NOTE

The number of nurses who enter the profession with diplomas in nursing has declined. Indeed, according to the AACN, diploma programs now comprise less than 10% of registered nurse programs (as cited in AACN, 2011). For this reason, diploma-prepared nurses are not discussed in this book.

The 2010 IOM report recommends that all nurses—regardless of educational level—use their training to practice to the fullest extent possible. Nurses are expected to become leaders and to develop and use knowledge regarding business practices that can help improve health. Despite the recommendation that 80% of nurses should have baccalaureate degrees by 2020, many believe that the associate degree will remain intact (Orsolini-Hain, 2012).

Nurses with ADNs differ from their counterparts with baccalaureate degrees in a variety of demographic characteristics—for example, whether they work full or part time, how long they have been working, and their age (McIntosh, Rambur, Val Palumbo, & Mongeon, 2003). Another much larger study that built on this work found that among recent graduates (0–5 years), baccalaureate-prepared nurses (BSNs) tended to be younger than associate degree-prepared nurses. ADN nurses were also less likely than BSN nurses to work full time and to seek work in Magnet hospitals. In addition, ADN nurses perceived less peer and unit support within their work environments than did BSN nurses (Sexton, Hunt, Cox, Teasley, & Carroll, 2008). In light of these findings, and of the changes taking place in nursing, it is important to hear from these nurses themselves about how they view their educational preparation and their nursing practice.

NOTE

For the purposes of this chapter, "ADN" refers to the associate degree in nursing or the associate of applied science degree.

Background

The ADN emerged in the 1950s in response to the demand for college-educated nurses as opposed to the traditional hospital (diploma) education. Another contributor to the emergence of the ADN was the concern that hospitals were using paraprofessionals instead of nurses because they could not find nurses to hire. Although baccalaureate programs did exist in those days, they did not graduate enough nurses in a short period of time. At the same time, there was an increased focus on community college education. Eventually, nursing education in these two-year colleges was proposed and implemented (Orsolini-Hain & Waters, 2009).

Initially, ADN programs attracted nontraditional students—partly because many could not get into or attend hospital-based programs and partly because tuition was considerably less than for other programs. Community colleges were often very accessible, and graduates typically remained in the same geographic area to work after graduation (Orsolini-Hain & Waters, 2009). ADN nurses were meant to practice technical (rather than professional) nursing, and associate-degree programs weren't intended to compete with other nursing programs. The associate degree was supposed to replace the diploma, and ADN nurses were expected to be members of a team that included professional or baccalaureate-prepared nurses (Orsolini-Hain & Waters, 2009). ADN-prepared nurses were placed in leadership and management roles. When they excelled in those roles, curricula were changed to incorporate formal preparation in leadership and management. Later, the profession began to expect that these nurses would go on to acquire BSNs (Orsolini-Hain & Waters, 2009).

For decades, controversy has continued regarding whether each role is distinct and should remain in nursing or whether the BSN should be the only entry-level degree. Regardless of what professional associations or state licensure boards wanted, in practice, ADNs and BSNs were used interchangeably in many cases (Orsolini-Hain & Waters, 2009). Indeed, in 2008, approximately 36% of nurses had an associate degree as their highest level of nursing education (HRSA, 2010). It appears that for the foreseeable future, the role is here to stay. Therefore, it is important to understand how ADN-prepared nurses view their preparation to begin work as new nurses and the nursing experience.

Preparation

Overall, the ADN graduates surveyed for this book said they felt they were well prepared for their nursing roles. Despite this, they also described various challenges they faced in their new nursing roles and gave suggestions as to how they could have been better prepared. Some were very specific about what they felt prepared to do and not do. The longer they had been practicing, the less likely ADN-prepared nurses were to qualify their answers when asked if they felt they were well prepared. For example, one nurse, who had been out of school less than 3 months, remarked, "Yes, I am prepared for Foley [catheter] insertions, medication passes, suctioning assessments, etc." In contrast, when asked if they felt prepared, several nurses who had graduated 13 to 18 months before simply responded "Yes."

It is interesting, however, to explore the responses of nurses, as they provide insight into how they perceived their level of preparation. A minority of nurses, regardless of how long they had been in nursing, responded with an emphatic "No" or, as one nurse said, "No, I felt completely lost."

Another nurse elaborated:

As far as skills and knowledge for an entry-level position, yes, but I really lacked the ability to manage a whole assignment. I wish we did more of that in nursing school. Having one patient or maybe two is not realistic.

As yet another nurse said, "Yes, but I think we should have been able to take an entire assignment at some point [in school] to see what it was like to have five to seven patients on our own." It is interesting that this continues to be an issue, as I remember feeling this way shortly after I graduated from nursing school in 1981.

Concern about inadequate clinical preparation was a common thread among all the nurses surveyed, regardless of how long ago they graduated. They shared the frustration that taking care of two to three patients while in school did not prepare them well to manage many more patients after they graduated. Lack of confidence and a limited sense of independence or autonomy were seen as the consequences of inadequate clinical preparation:

> [I felt prepared] to a degree. I felt I understood the basics of nursing and what is expected of me as an employee. However, I don't feel my clinical skills were ready, which I know comes with time and experience. I feel nurses should have more rotations a week or learn all of the book stuff up front and then spend the rest of the semester working in a hospital, so you can really develop your skills and confidence.

While expressing a general feeling of being prepared, nurses had concerns about specific aspects of nursing work for which they felt less prepared than for others. One nurse said, "Information-wise, yes [I felt prepared], but patient load and calling doctors and talking to families—no." Another nurse commented, "Yes, for the most part [I felt prepared]. I still will have a lot of nerves going when I start my career but I am willing to learn." A third nurse said, "I think I have a good foundation to build upon. However, nothing can really prepare you for the fast pace and time-management skills needed in the hospital."

According to the nurses surveyed, clinical preparation not only includes caring for patients, but also how to communicate with physicians and staff, how to chart correctly, and above all, how to manage time efficiently and effectively. As several nurses commented, time management and charting "can be overwhelming" and require practice.

GRADUATES FEEL UNDERPREPARED

According to survey responses, ADN-prepared nurses feel underprepared in the following areas:

- *Clinical skills*
- *Managing a large patient load*
- *Communicating with physicians*
- *Time management*
- *Charting*
- *Leadership and delegation*

Nursing Education

Nurses who responded to the survey suggested several ways their nursing education might have better prepared them to begin as new nurses. Specifically, nurses indicated that they would have benefited from the following:

- Instruction on time management and documentation
- Clinical experience
- Instruction on leadership and delegation
- Instruction on communication
- Pursuit of a BSN

Time Management and Documentation

Nurses who graduated in the previous 1 to 3 months placed particular emphasis on the need for more training in time management and documentation. One nurse said, "More documentation, even if I had to put it on paper and hand it in to an instructor, it would have helped me with time management as I began my orientation." Another agreed that time management needed to be taught, but wondered if one could *ever* be prepared for hospital work: "I think I was well prepared. The rest will be just job training. Can you teach time management that you need in a fast-paced hospital? I don't think you can!"

Several nurses also mentioned charting, noting that they should have received more practice doing it while in school. One nurse wrote, "I would like to have had the experience of doing the actual charting that is required of the nurse; as students we're only allowed to do this CNA (certified nurse's aide) charting."

Clinical Experience

Nurses with ADNs overwhelmingly supported the need for more clinical experience while in school. One nurse commented that "more clinical hours with smaller clinical groups" would have been helpful. Another said, "[In the] last semester, we should have more to do or a heavier patient load to learn time management." Yet another nurse was more specific and described needing "more clinical experience talking with doctors and a larger patient load." Another nurse agreed: "[We need] more assigned patients in clinical. One or two is not realistic."

One nurse was much more specific:

I would change the educational system. I would make a model similar to med[ical] school—one where you focus on the books and learning up front and then move into the hospital for weeks at a time instead of getting one or two clinical rotations a week. I don't feel you really have an opportunity to become fully prepared and develop your skills when you only spend one 12-hour shift a week there.

Nurses mentioned other aspects of clinical education as being necessary to prepare the novice nurse. One nurse cited the need to practice more mock codes, whereas another suggested more pediatric experiences. A third nurse wrote, "Clinicals in areas outside the hospital would be helpful: home care, doctor's offices, nursing homes/short-term rehab, methadone clinics, etc." (Nursing schools tend to provide the bulk of the clinical experiences in hospitals or other inpatient facilities.)

NOTE

In my experience, nursing students who are still in school are more interested in acute-care experiences than in community-based experiences. Indeed, after having community-based experiences, many are amazed that such clinical work is so interesting and challenging. Many do not appreciate how much a community-based nurse needs to know, and that nurses in a community setting work much more independently than those in an acute-care facility. It is perhaps a disservice to students that nursing schools don't provide more of these experiences while students are in school.

Another nurse argued that clinical assignments while in school could be arranged differently to better prepare the nurse:

I wish in our last year we actually took whole assignments and worked side-by-side with a nurse from the hospital where we did our clinicals. Ten students to one instructor makes it hard to do the job the primary nurse actually does. Instead, we became glorified CNAs who could give meds.

It is worth considering whether nursing students get everything possible out of their clinical experiences or whether, as "warm bodies"—especially in their last year, when they are the most knowledgeable as students—they are needed to act in ancillary roles to help the unit. Are final-year students given enough practice in the roles they will have when they begin their first job? Could their clinical experiences in the final year be structured differently to more closely resemble their future roles as novice nurses?

One nurse felt clinical experiences in school should be more challenging, suggesting that "clinicals have more challenge [regarding the] pathophysiology of [the] patient's condition rather than so much [emphasis on] task orientation." Another nurse put it this way:

> *We seemed to be short on experiences, and I look back and know that the clinical portion of my nursing program did not fill that gap. I know every case is different, but during nursing school, the clinical lacked those life scenarios that put you in a situation where you have to use your nursing judgment. Doing vitals, giving baths, and assisting with ambulation is fine, but there's much more than that when you are standing behind the nurse's station. I feel our clinical experience should have included certain skills to better prepare nursing students to do the function that you're intended to do.*

NOTE

Interestingly, the view of educational preparation from nurses who had been out of school for more than 1 year focused on the less tangible aspects of nursing, whereas the nurses more recently out of school seemed to care more about practicing tangible skills.

Leadership and Delegation

In addition to requiring more clinical experience, nurses requested that there be more in-depth education on leadership and delegation while in nursing school. One nurse wrote, "[I would like] more on role delegation, how to work with PCAs (patient care assistants), [more on] time management." Another mentioned that "classes on leadership and the practice acts in the state where I went to school" would have been helpful.

Communication

Communication was another issue mentioned—especially among nurses who had graduated 1 to 3 months previously. As one nurse put it, "I would have liked to learn more about what to communicate and who to communicate it to."

> **NOTE**
>
> *The issue of communication is discussed further later in this chapter.*

The BSN

Overall, nurses believed they would have been better served if they had gotten BSNs rather than ADNs. They seemed to think that if they had gotten bachelor's degrees in nursing instead of associate degrees, they might have been better prepared for their roles. In fact, most of the nurses surveyed had already decided they would need to begin work on their baccalaureate degrees, because they could see the value in having the BSN.

One nurse said, "Since I had a previous bachelor's degree, I should have done the accelerated BSN; it would've taken less time than the AAS (associate of applied science)." Another nurse agreed: "I would have gone straight into a BSN upgrade program; the longer I wait, the harder it gets to get back into schooling." One nurse remarked, "I wish I had the opportunity to attend school much earlier. At times, I wonder if a 4-year college would've made a difference." Another nurse thought that adding training in advanced cardiac life support (ACLS) and pediatric advanced life support (PALS) would make nurses "more desirable in the job market."

Barriers and Challenges

ADN-prepared nurses talked about the barriers encountered as they tried to adjust to their roles as new nurses. Not surprisingly, they were numerous. They included the following:

- Limited employment opportunities
- Making the transition from student to nurse
- Managing one's time

- Dealing with a perceived lack of professional status
- Handling various everyday tasks
- Politics

ADDITIONAL BARRIERS AND CHALLENGES FOR THE NEW NURSE

In addition to those listed, new nurses face the following barriers and challenges:

- *Talking to families*
- *Learning about the facility and organization*
- *Working 12-hour shifts*
- *Workflow*
- *Multitasking*
- *Handling the fast pace*
- *Standing up for themselves*

Limited Employment Opportunities

The nurses who responded to the survey conducted for this book were surprised by how difficult it was to find a job. One nurse stated, "After completing my ADN, the biggest adjustment was being able to find employment; almost all hospitals wanted nurses with at least 2 years' experience." Other nurses echoed the same lament, such as the one who wrote, "New grad positions are limited and hundreds of people apply to them. I'm finding with the openings, they still want you to have experience, and if you don't you will not get the job." Difficulty finding a job during the current economic climate can be demoralizing. One nurse, who had been out of school 7 to 12 months, responded, "The lack of full-time jobs is disheartening. There is a lot of part-time work available, and fortunately I've been able to make full-time work out of three part-time jobs."

Another nurse explained:

I'm a recent nurse graduate. After graduating and soon there-after, taking the state boards, I was...overjoyed and excited because [of] the future that was ahead of me. Unfortunately, the change in the economy placed the burden on new hires; besides the economy, it seemed I was lacking experience and the clinical experience [I had in school] wasn't enough. Competition out there was much greater than I was ready to face. It took some persuasion on my part and soon I found myself with a job—not a dream job nor a position I had aspired to hold, but I'm happy to say that I'm glad I wake up in the morning and go out into the nursing world with an open mind and a warm heart.

One nurse said:

I thought that being that we are in the midst of the nursing shortage and I had experience working as an LPN, I'd be able to find a job right away. No companies in [my state] seem to want to hire new grads. It would rather pay overtime to their experienced nurses.

Another expressed distress regarding the financial remuneration of doing the job of a nurse: "I love what I do, but I thought I'd be able to support my family and be more comfortable financially."

A third nurse was unable to obtain a job in a hospital despite expecting to be able to do so right out of school:

I did not expect to be working in an office, but I'm grateful for the opportunity to really get to know patients and develop a professional, caring relationship with them. I find myself wanting to help people more and more. At the end of the day I feel good about what I'm doing, and I think this is important for any job you have.

Transitioning From Student to Nurse

The transition from being a student to being a nurse is challenging. One nurse remarked on the difficulty of "transitioning to being the nurse, not having the nurse/professor to rely on; having to ask colleagues for guidance." Another nurse agreed that it was difficult "not knowing what to do in certain situations. Seasoned nurses [were] not treating me the same [as they did other nurses]."

Clinical experiences while in school did not prepare new nurses for the large patient load they would find, especially in a hospital setting. As one nurse said:

> Going from two to three patients in clinical to six patients and keeping up with the documentation hourly [was difficult]. Orders change constantly. It becomes a little overwhelming, but I am getting more confident as the weeks pass.

Once again, while a common theme was a concern about insufficient clinical experience prior to graduation, a lack of knowledge or confidence in the other aspects of clinical work compounded the challenges of adapting to the role. One nurse explained, "Learning to manage a team of patients on my own [was hard]. Learning the ins and outs of everything you did not have to do in nursing school: Phoning doctors, talking to family, and learning a new hospital [were all challenging]."

One nurse cited the lack of clinical experience as a barrier to transition. "I felt our clinical experience while in nursing school should've included certain skills to better prepare us to handle functions that we are intended and expected to do." Another nurse stated emphatically, "In clinical, we only had one patient at a time! The real world doesn't work that way." Learning to adapt to 12-hour shifts, not to mention "learning everything about a new hospital including the computer system, the people, the night shift, and then having to take care of patients at the same time," can be overwhelming for new nurses.

Time Management

Just learning to manage one's time was a major challenge for new nurses. Indeed, one nurse mentioned this first among a long list of concerns: "time management, decision-making, learning how to work with physicians, charting, not enough preparation as a student, not enough orientation." However, another nurse viewed overcoming these difficulties as par for the course: "Independence and confidence—in nursing school, [we were] told these feelings were part of the normal transition into nursing after graduating. It's not something you can be prepared for."

Experienced nurses have a hard time empathizing with the energy and concentration needed in a new job (especially in a new profession), the difficulty in understanding the sometimes overwhelming paperwork involved, and the difficulty even in learning and understanding the language of nursing. It may be hard for them to remember the difficulties presented when learning how to handle an entire assignment, adjusting to working night shifts, and learning the legal intricacies of working in health care. The challenges of learning many new things at once are compounded by attempts to grasp how to manage one's time and prioritize one's work. Being able to multitask to manage all the tasks required of the nurse is a skill for which some nurses do not feel prepared. As one new nurse said, "Trying to get everything done. I think it is critical to be able to multitask or you'll sink."

As the new nurse gains experience and conquers some of these early challenges, independence and confidence in the role emerge. One nurse, who had been out of school 19 to 24 months, cited the major barriers as being "finding a job, learning how to delegate, and standing up for myself." Standing up for oneself—especially when communicating with physicians—is indeed a challenge. Nurses also struggle with learning their own boundaries and when to ask others for help. As one nurse, who graduated 1 to 3 months prior, said, "One challenge that I struggle with is should I call the MD (medical doctor) and advocate for the patient or am I overstepping my boundaries?" As time goes on, however, nurses begin to develop intuition and learn to trust their own instincts. A nurse who had been out of school for 7 to 12 months said, "I work with a lot of new doctors, so I need to learn to trust my instincts to know when something's really wrong." Another nurse, who had been out of school 13 to 18 months, agreed: "The most challenging things were learning to work with physicians and asking for help when I need it; after working for a year, I feel much more confident in the skills."

One nurse described the biggest challenge as "becoming more comfortable being 'the nurse,' understanding the complexities of the nurse's role and responsibilities within my specific environment." Another nurse described this as "putting the pieces together from textbook to real human."

> **NOTE**
>
> *The ability to apply what was learned from textbooks and limited clinical experiences in school, and to distinguish what works in theory from what actually happens in practice, is indicative of a healthy and successful transition into the role of the nurse. It is important that new nurses be able to move from the very concrete adjustments of learning paperwork and policies to being able to integrate the meaning of nursing into how they see themselves. This is key to seeing oneself as a nurse rather than as a person performing the role of a nurse.*

Lack of Professional Status

One nurse lamented, "Nursing does not feel nearly as fair [as my previous profession] and the individuals are less mature and professional. It's clique-y." Another nurse discussed "the isolation that exists in the acute care setting. It is so fast-paced, the nurse has no time to interact with management as a professional. The nurse is not seen as a professional."

Indeed, the field of nursing has struggled to be viewed as a profession since its inception. Many argue that having so many different entry levels into practice stymie any attempt by nursing to be seen as a profession on par with medical doctors or lawyers. In addition, nurses may be at the bedside or not and still be considered nurses. Those at the bedside often view those who do not perform patient care as imposters, while nurses in academia or research express disdain for nurses who do not "move beyond" the bedside. (This issue is discussed in more detail in Chapter 6, "The Chasm in Nursing.") Nurses who come from other professions may be surprised to see how nurses treat each other and the confusion patients often experience when trying to sort out who is the nurse and who is not.

Furthermore, nurses with associate degrees may feel even more marginalized, particularly by other nurses. The public is rarely able to differentiate the ADN-prepared from the BSN-prepared nurse. However, the profession in general tends to offer little respect to the ADN nurse, which is unwarranted and unfair, particularly because they have the same responsibilities as BSN-prepared nurses, are often paid the same, and are frequently aware that they need to progress in their education.

NOTE

Professional organizations, particularly those involved in research, do not tend to target associate degree-prepared nurses for recruitment or membership. These organizations do not typically view ADN nurses as having the knowledge or preparation to participate in or understand nursing research. But how, then, can ADN nurses be expected to apply research to practice—especially in light of the current emphasis on evidence-based practice? It is vital that ADN nurses be taught to read and critically review the literature so they can apply research to practice. ADN nurses must also advance to the baccalaureate degree and beyond so they can become full participants in every aspect of the profession—and not be excluded from the more scholarly endeavors of nursing.

Day-to-Day Work

New nurses can find the day-to-day work of being a nurse very challenging. As one nurse put it, there is "lots of paperwork for discharge and placing orders [from] the doctor. I wasn't prepared for that part." Simply learning to deal with the stress of short staffing and inadequate resources is also difficult, as is mastering specific skills such as intravenous line skills and performing various procedures.

Of course, on top of all that, the new nurse must also learn to manage an entire assignment of patients. This becomes even more difficult for the nurse who is required to float to another unit or setting. One fortunate nurse said, "I am a float nurse and I feel very prepared for the role given my educational experience." In contrast, another said, "Pharmacology is a challenge and I don't feel fully prepared." Both of these nurses had been practicing for 7 to 12 months; perhaps the difference was the specific preparation they received from their associate-degree programs.

NOTE

A lack of experience can make it difficult to manage the long hours, increased number of patients, documentation, and day-to-day work required as a nurse regardless of setting.

Politics

Nurses who work for large or bureaucratic organizations may not feel that they get the one-on-one attention they need when they start out on the job. In addition, one nurse noted that "putting up with the politics of working for a large corporation" is a challenge—one for which many new nurses are not prepared. Another nurse viewed this problem from a larger perspective: "The economy and the new health care law will be a challenge for all present and new nurses. It is my impression that nurses will have to be diligent in the political arena to make sure our voices are heard."

> **NOTE**
>
> *Keeping current with the politics and changes in the profession will help the associate-degree nurse feel more confident that furthering one's education in nursing can lead to more nursing opportunities, both clinically and outside of direct patient care.*

Facilitators

The survey asked whether new nurses encountered anything or anyone that helped them adjust and adapt to their new roles. Overwhelmingly, these novice nurses saw having a preceptor or another nurse who was willing to mentor them—either formally or informally—as integral to a positive and happy adjustment. One nurse said, "My mentor helped me learn techniques that help me do my job and she helped me begin to learn how to manage my time." Another nurse said that the preceptor, as well as "taking one thing at a time," assisted the transition.

> **NOTE**
>
> *Unfortunately, many new nurses do not receive mentoring from more experienced nurses. As one nurse said, "The challenge I face is not having enough experience to back me up. There are other nurses that are more experienced; some don't like to train or share their thoughts because they feel threatened." The quality of orientation and whether a nurse has a mentor can significantly affect the nurse's ability to adapt to the new role.*

Respondents also noted that talking with other new nurses helped provide support and the knowledge that the barriers and challenges encountered were not unique to their own experience. One nurse commented on the role of "a great support system, from my friends in nursing school to the new people I met on the job."

Nurses also saw the opportunity to frequently review policies and procedures and to build relationships with colleagues as instrumental. One nurse remarked upon "the supportive colleagues, feeling comfortable enough to ask for help where/when [it was] needed." Another nurse said, "I found a place that is willing to work with me and shape me into the real nurse I'm becoming."

Many respondents saw a residency program as particularly helpful. As one new nurse stated, "My workplace has a nursing residency program. I feel at ease knowing they won't just throw me onto the floor without knowing what I am doing." Overall, long training periods, help from experienced nurses (particularly preceptors), and one-on-one mentorship were the most important facilitators to a good adjustment. Those facilitators and "buying well-made shoes" seemed to be very important.

Interestingly, one nurse spoke of having a first job in a doctor's office and how this was helping in transitioning into the role of the nurse:

I'm not working in a hospital. Instead I was able to get a job at a doctor's office, which is really helping me develop my role with patients. Plus, I am going on to get my BSN and continue to seek certification in other areas. I keep learning, researching, and reading the ANA (American Nurses Association) newsletter to stay abreast of nursing.

NOTE

An appreciation for lifelong learning is a gift that all educators hope to pass along to their students. It is important that nurses with associate-degree preparation view their schooling as a stepping-stone to higher education in nursing.

FACILITATORS FOR THE NEW NURSE
The following are key facilitators for new nurses: • *A good preceptor/mentor* • *A solid support system* • *A long training period*

Summary

This chapter has presented the concerns ADN-prepared recent graduates have about their preparation for their new roles and the barriers and facilitators they have encountered. (Interestingly, BSN-prepared recent graduates share many of the same perceptions and concerns, as you will see in Chapter 3.) While many said they felt prepared, these recent graduates also expressed the wish that they had had more clinical experience, including heavier patient loads and more lessons in documentation, taking orders, giving report, and communicating with physicians and staff. Time management also appeared to be a priority. If nurses can learn how to prioritize and manage time in school, they are more likely to be able to adjust to the demands of fast-paced clinical environments.

Although learning basic and advanced clinical skills and techniques is important, nurses should also be taught the more intangible aspects of nursing: dealing with families, helping patients cope with illness or imminent death, and strong communication skills. ADN-prepared nurses also seemed to want more practice with leadership and delegation skills. Although ADN-prepared nurses were not intended to undertake leadership roles, they are and should be prepared to take them on. Nursing students should learn how a registered nurse functions and not be made to document or function like a CNA or an LPN.

Chapter 2

Life As an ADN-Prepared Nurse

Chapter 1 addressed the preparation for beginning work as a new nurse and some of the barriers, challenges, and facilitators that ADN recent graduates tend to encounter. These respondents also made suggestions about how their education might have been improved to better prepare them. This chapter delves into their experiences once in the role of a new nurse, how the meaning of nursing may or may not have changed for them, and their advice for graduating students and other new nurses.

Orientation to the Role

The 2010 Institute of Medicine report specifies that organizations should implement residency programs to assist the transition of nurses in new roles. Although this need not apply only to new nurses, implementation can potentially help new ADN-prepared nurses to have smoother transitions (Orsolini-Hain, 2012).

There appears to be a great deal of variation in how much orientation new nurses with associate-degree preparation receive. Some nurses do not get a formal orientation, whereas others may have a mentor or preceptor for varying lengths of time. It seems clear that having a lengthy orientation or extended time with a preceptor can make a big difference in how well a nurse adapts to the new role.

Preceptors and Mentors

The quality of the orientation and of the preceptor is very important. One nurse, who had been a nurse for 7 to 12 months, commented, "I am in long-term care. I got a month [of orientation] working with LPNs (licensed practical nurses)." In contrast, another nurse stated, "I went into an intense 3-month internship, an orientation program. [The] internship was very specific to the job/department and it was run by the nurse educator of the department. I felt like I was still in school: Readings, lectures, tasks, etc., along with bedside orientation with a mentor during the internship." A 10- to 16-week orientation is not uncommon among nurses. Those who had long orientation periods were more likely to report that they felt prepared when they started their jobs.

Orientations differ widely. One nurse talked about a 10-week competence-based orientation program designed to ensure exposure to a number of different clinical experiences. Another described the following:

> *I had 1 week of in-class orientation; they basically reviewed policy/procedures and the computer program. I had 4 weeks of the preceptor during the day shift, 1 week without [the] preceptor, and 2 weeks with a preceptor on the evening shift. RNs were always available to answer questions and for support.*

One nurse talked about receiving orientation with several different nurses, both on day shift and night shift: "Then, my first day, I had five patients to care for, and three students to mentor! [Having] three patients for a couple of weeks would have been better and no students to deal with at first, since I was still trying to figure out my own routine." Unfortunately, pressures to get new nurses onboard and ready to care for patients independently may lead to situations of "the blind leading the blind," with new nurses, just off their own orientation periods, being asked to mentor or precept other nurses. This is unfair and potentially unsafe for both the nurses and their patients and should not continue. A more acceptable scenario is that of the nurse who received "1 week of hospital orientation and 1 week of nursing orientation as well as 12 weeks of precepting with the nurse on the floor. [The nurse received] 6 weeks on days and 6 weeks on nights"—the shift for which the nurse was originally hired.

Another nurse talked about "mostly staying with the same nurse every day. [I] also got oriented with the unit secretary, nursing tech, and admission and discharge nurses." Orientation with people who work in other areas within the agency can help the new nurse establish his or her bearings and feel more comfortable about asking others for help as time goes on. It is crucial that the new nurse understand what the support staff does and how other specialty nurses fit into the overall mission and procedures within the institution. Knowing the duties of ancillary staff and professionals from other disciplines can help the nurse see how to provide holistic nursing care and can prevent the new nurse from causing friction with others out of ignorance of professional boundaries and expectations.

One nurse described a very in-depth orientation:

I had 8 weeks of mentorship that in the beginning focused on getting to know the MDs (medical doctors), PAs (physician assistants), my fellow nurses, and nurse's aides on the floor, first. Secondly, we've been focused on understanding the disease process of our patients to understand the type of medical and nursing care provided on the floor. During my 8 weeks, we discussed time management and prioritizing patient care needs to effectively give good quality care to all patients.

Other nurses described being especially pleased with the mentorship and orientation they received. As one nurse said, "[I] had an awesome mentor who helped me understand how to be a good nurse. She gave constructive criticism and helped me grow. Although 8 weeks seems like not enough time." Another said, "I was given excellent training in order to prepare me for my role as an RN." Whereas one nurse was not happy that the orientation was 7 weeks and described it as "too long," another nurse seemed pleased that the 6-month fellowship she was completing working directly with a mentor would help improve her job opportunities in the future.

One nurse discussed the orientation period:

I received 2 months of orientation, where I shadowed nurses and was encouraged to ask questions. An additional 2 weeks were offered for new graduates, which included going over policies and procedures and having the opportunity to talk to other undergrads.

Several comments were not so positive. One nurse described receiving no mentoring at all. Another, who worked in a nursing home, received little orientation and felt that "the bulk of [orientation] is on-the-job, as-you-go learning." A third nurse talked about being hired for the emergency room but receiving orientation in the fast track (an area of the hospital that takes semi-urgent emergency room patients): "When orientation was complete, I was expected to work in both places; it was awful to go from semi-urgent to emergent patients overnight."

Peers and Colleagues

In addition to excellent preceptors and mentors, many of the new nurses surveyed were fortunate to have peers and colleagues who welcomed them and were willing to answer their questions and offer assistance. As one nurse commented, "They're very supportive and I can go to them with whatever I need." Another said of the more experienced nurses: "They are used to it. They know how undergrads are." A third nurse echoed this feeling: "They realized what I knew and helped me a lot." Still another nurse said this: "Everyone has been really supportive and helpful. All say they still ask questions to this day."

> **NOTE**
>
> *It is important that all nurses feel they can ask questions. In a profession in which patient safety is the primary concern, nurses must acknowledge that one cannot know everything, and that it is better to ask than to potentially jeopardize the safety of a patient. Regardless of length of time or experience in nursing, nurses are always learning—or should be, anyway. The inability to accept that things could be done in a different or better way hampers progress. Nurses should encourage each other to ask questions and to pursue better ways of doing things. This is one of the hallmarks of the true nursing professional.*

Although nurses may feel welcomed by some peers and colleagues, they may not feel welcomed by others—in some cases, this includes administrators. One very new nurse commented, "I think it just depends on the individual. Some are very helpful and others are not. My saying is that nurses eat their young." Interestingly, another new nurse said, "I have not had any problems except for a few nurses who have forgotten they were new once. Maybe [that] should be part of [the] coursework... mentoring the new nurse."

> **NOTE**
>
> *In recent years, much has been made in the literature on the "nurses eat their young" mentality. In response, some nursing schools have begun including lessons that teach nurses to empathize with and support each other. Lessons on how to be a good mentee, as well as how to mentor others, might help refine and shape the expectations that experienced and novice nurses have about each other.*

One nurse said, "Most people are very nice and helpful, while others don't really acknowledge me. It's to be expected." Another nurse explained, "Seasoned RNs (over 10 years of experience) act like they don't have time to teach me the ropes. Others who have graduated within the last 10 years are much more welcoming." Another went a bit further: "Most people were very supportive but there are a number of nurses who have no tolerance for new nurses."

> **NOTE**
>
> *The new nurse should be reassured that in the beginning, it is normal to feel overwhelmed. That being said, the expectation is that new nurses will ask questions and use resources to fill the gaps in their preparation. Helping new nurses get up to speed should be a partnership between the new nurse and the experienced people with whom that new nurse interacts. The experienced people should display patience with someone new and encourage questions and observations; at the same time, new nurses should be eager and motivated to do their homework and make the effort to learn what they do not know rather than waiting for others to teach it to them.*

One nurse explained, "As the weeks go by, I'm feeling more comfortable and confident about doing what I'm expected to do; every day that goes by, I learn something new. My colleagues make me feel like I'm part of the team." While another nurse felt that most colleagues had been supportive and understanding, "there are some who forget what it is like to be a new graduate nurse. My supervisors are nothing but supportive and encouraging."

Having a manager who promotes teamwork and encourages experienced nurses to support new nurses seems critical to ensuring that new nurses have a good experience while adjusting to the role. As one nurse said, "My managers encourage an atmosphere of teamwork, mentorship, and friendship." Another nurse, however, felt that the day shift staff and management were not as helpful as those on the night shift. This nurse attributed that to the fact that there were many more new graduates on the night shift than on the day shift. Regarding her nurse manager, another nurse commented, "The nurse manager felt I was too 'soft' and cared about my patients too much." But, the same nurse continued, "My preceptor said he found it refreshing to see someone care." One nurse, who started in nursing a little bit later than most, stated that "Most are very helpful; however, I felt judged and hazed by some of the younger nurses."

Communicating With Physicians and Staff

Communication appears to be a common difficulty among recently graduated nurses with associate-degree preparation:

> Every facility is different, and I can count the times when I felt that I was back in school. I had to learn charting, taking orders, transcribing orders, handling new admissions, discharging patients, and dealing with a loss, as well as multitasking, especially when you're doing med[ication] passes, etc. Most importantly, I had to get over the fear of talking to physicians and the family.

Difficulty learning how to communicate with physicians was common regardless of how long the nurse had been out of school. As one nurse said, "Some are more approachable than others. I am at a teaching hospital and just when I get comfortable with them they rotate." Another remarked, "Yes, they are just people too. I try to learn as much as I can from them." With regard to communicating with physicians and other staff, one nurse said, "[I am] getting there but that is the hardest part of the job some days."

The ability to communicate with physicians, staff, patients, and families seems to improve over time, but survey responses indicate that nurses could benefit from more practice communicating with these entities while in school. A nurse who had been working for 7 to 12 months said that for the most part, she was comfortable talking with physicians and staff. "I am still a little intimidated," she added, "but I grow more comfortable with each encounter." Another nurse, who had been out of school for approximately the same amount of time, said, "I had to get over the fear of talking to physicians and the family and I had to get over the fear of talking to other health professionals but now I've shown great confidence."

One nurse remarked:

Since I work at a teaching hospital, I have to deal with a lot of first-year interns. When I started nights (shift), I would call the intern and they didn't always have the answers. They would say, "I'm new!" And I would say, "So am I!" It gets easier the longer you are there and the closer you get to your team.

Having some experience working in other fields before entering nursing seems to better prepare the new nurse for communicating with physicians. One nurse commented, "I was also comfortable in the hospital setting talking to [physicians]. I have a background in genetics and cell biology, so this allows me [to] communicate with them or on their level." One nurse commented, "The physicians in our department are wonderful and supportive. This is the only place I've worked, so I've only this experience to offer." A second nurse noted:

I am comfortable working with them now. In the beginning there was a lot of fear of appearing stupid for not knowing basic things about my patient. As time has gone on I've become more familiar with the type of patients my floor takes care of and I've become more comfortable in my knowledge about my patient care.

Most of the nurses responded that they felt comfortable working with other staff and communicating with them. However, supervising others such as nurses' aides was a noted challenge. Over time, it appears that nurses develop confidence in communicating with both physicians and staff. One nurse said, "Dietary, social workers, PAs, OTs (occupational therapists), PTs (physical therapists), respiratory, are all friendly and approachable."

Role Change

When asked if they felt that their expectations of their role in nursing had changed since graduating and beginning a new job, new nurses gave varied answers. One nurse remarked, "Somewhat. I had hoped to have more time for one-on-one patient interaction, and I have six patients to care for, so I'm always rushing to pass meds, do two assessments a shift, and get all of my charting done." Another nurse stated, "Expectations are much greater than I had anticipated. However, I feel confident that I will be able to get through it."

NOTE

Most of the nurses surveyed—especially those with the least experience in the profession—were overwhelmed by the detail-oriented nature of nursing work. They were not prepared for the paperwork and appeared to have underestimated what was involved in being a nurse. Adjusting to the pace of the hospital environment was especially difficult, as was having limited time to develop relationships with patients—both unexpected findings for new nurses. As one nurse said, "You really have to know what you're doing."

Despite the trials and tribulations, most nurses said they were happy with their choice to become nurses. As one nurse stated, "Most days, yes [I am happy]...Sometimes when I'm overwhelmed, I second-guess myself, but usually the next day is much better." Others said they get a tremendous sense of accomplishment from being a nurse. One nurse noted, "I originally planned on medical school but the opportunity presented itself [to become a] nurse. I must say I'm really enjoying it so far. The nursing profession is still wide open and will continue to grow and there are numerous opportunities out there to pursue."

Several others spoke of the desire to pursue further education in nursing and the recognition that doing so would enhance their knowledge and their careers in the future. As one nurse summarized, "I'm extremely happy and I hope to continue to further my education." Another said, "I am happy to be a nurse but I'm moving on to a new level of nursing." Others said that they were not happy or had mixed feelings about being a nurse. Still others were undecided about how they felt about being in nursing.

> *I'm working in a very fast-paced department where I don't have much time to develop relationships. I think I will need to find a better fit for my personality and what I want/need from the profession.*

The Meaning of Nursing

The new nurses surveyed were asked to discuss whether their views about the profession or the meaning of nursing had changed for them since graduation. Responses were varied. Some felt their views had not changed; nursing was largely what they had expected it would be. Many had anticipated that it would be very rewarding and a lot of hard work, and it turned out to be that way.

> *I always knew that nursing is what I wanted to do. I was a CNA prior to becoming a nurse, so I had a feel for what it was like from that perspective. Nursing is much harder and physically draining but the difference one makes in others' lives is priceless.*

Others mentioned that the profession of nursing was undervalued and that nurses could do more to bring recognition to the profession. As one nurse said, "Nursing is struggling to become professional." Another said, "We are underpaid." A third nurse said, "My views haven't changed. I just have even more respect for the profession and those who are good at what they do."

Some of the nurses surveyed had come to respect the profession more since graduating. They loved it despite the struggles to adjust because they find it rewarding. As one nurse put it, "I think it is an amazing profession. Being able to help others is a noble career. I do, however, wish there was less paperwork." The rewards seemed to outweigh the difficulties.

Others felt disillusioned. One nurse stated, "I used to think patients would be thankful for the care they received. Now I know most think they expect the best care possible while being rude, inconsiderate, and demanding." Another reported, "In the beginning, the nursing profession seemed a piece of the puzzle of patient-centered care to me. It seems to me now that our care is more than that."

For some, time constraints have affected the way they view themselves as nurses. As one nurse stated, "Time constraints take away some things I'd like to do and politics make it hard to get a great idea or even evidence-based practice into play." However, as time goes on, becoming more comfortable in the profession can also help change nurses' views of it. One nurse explained, "I'm not as scared to go to work every day! Now that I know my team and I feel more comfortable in my role, things are much easier." However, peer support and collegiality can make a difference: "As with any field, you can feel disappointed in some of the nurses' attitudes to their peers."

When asked whether the meaning of nursing had changed for them since graduating from school, nurses echoed many of these same themes. One nurse said, "I thought of it as being a great job, now I think it's something I'm giving back to other people." Another stated enthusiastically, "I'm so honored to be in the nursing career and excited to begin my journey." A third remarked:

> Sad to say, documentation is a big part of nursing, which leaves less time for the one-on-one. I would love to see that change. I wanted to be a nurse to help people, not to be on the computer. It's not balanced.

One brand-new nurse commented on the meaning of nursing in light of educational preparation: "In school, we learned a great deal about medical issues, pathophysiology. However, in the profession I deal a lot less with medical and much more with patient comfort, family, questions, concerns."

Interestingly, nurses who had been out of school 4 to 6 months viewed the meaning of nursing a little bit differently from their newer counterparts. One nurse said, "It is much more holistic and patient centered [than I had thought it would be]." Another said, "You have to get personally involved with the patients to give them the best care. You can't just leave those feelings at work." A third remarked:

Before I entered the program, I thought of nursing as very techni-cal. Now, I realize it is more about human connection and truly caring for your patients. They respond better to treatment and are more open to accepting changes in their life.

Other nurses who had been out of school 4 to 6 months expressed negative views. One nurse said, "I feel it's much more cutthroat and it's who you know rather than how competent you may be." Another said, "It is very complicated and functions on many levels: clerical, administrative, patient care, educator…. It is difficult to pull nursing to a level of professional when it is held back."

Nurses who had been out of school 7 to 12 months seemed to take a more philosophical view of the meaning of nursing and what it holds for them. Said one: "[The meaning of nursing] has been enhanced by caring for others, and having meaningful connections/interactions with patients. It's very powerful." Another said:

I personally gained respect from my colleagues and those in the healthcare field. The meaning of nursing is not valued by a lot of people and it needs to be acknowledged. We're the ones with patients 24/7, I feel we know them best.

To many, the meaning of nursing seemed to relate to the responses nurses get from patients. As one nurse said, "It depends on the kind of night you have, but it's such a good feeling when your patients feel that they can trust you and they can confide in you. Reminds you of why you chose the profession." Another said:

They value the art of nursing most. Just about anyone can be trained to do the tasks a nurse needs to do in a day. I most value the compassion and caring that a really good nurse is able to show her patients while doing the tasks. I changed my career to become a nurse for that reason. I want to help make a difference in someone's life…if even for a moment.

Nurses who had been in the field for 13 to 18 months talked about the stress involved in providing good nursing care. One such nurse said, "It's much more stressful but it's also much more rewarding than I could've imagined. It's a love/hate thing." Another noted, "Sometimes I feel like I am just a body to take a patient load. I wish I had time to truly give the kind of care I want and not feel like I am always working so understaffed." A third observed, "Nursing involves more emotional support that I previously thought."

Finally, nurses who'd been out of school 19 to 24 months, while still finding themselves surprised by some aspects of nursing, worried that they were experiencing some disillusionment. As one nurse said, "I don't know what it means to be a nurse anymore."

Advice

Surveyed nurses were asked to offer advice to those who are just beginning in nursing. Those nurses most recently out of school seemed to be reminding themselves, while telling others, that adjustment takes patience.

Don't be afraid to ask questions. Everyone is feeling the same, and it will get better. I was just told by a fellow nursing student that it's like learning to drive standard. As the new RN, you need to think before you put the clutch in and shift. Nursing is the same. We are thinking before each step and our fellow nurses are not even thinking about it. [For them] it is second nature.

It is important to ask questions and be willing to learn. As one nurse said, "Good luck. It's a hard course but I think it will be worth it." Another said, "Take it one day at a time and do your best. Try to find the nurse who would be helpful." A third said, "Have patience with yourself, and don't be afraid to ask questions." Overall, their simple message was, "Don't panic."

Nurses who had been out of school 4 to 6 months agree. As one nurse said: "Give it time, work out every day, you will get better at what you do, and ask questions. You will learn something every day, and that is what the veteran nurses on my floor say, they are still learning!"

Another nurse was more specific: "Make a list with checkboxes of everything that needs to be done for each patient so you don't forget anything. Also, be sure to constantly check orders."

Many nurses recommended continuing on for higher education in nursing. As one nurse said, "Keep learning and keep pushing forward. Do not give up on the lack of jobs. Find something, anything, that will help with experience."

Nurses who'd been in nursing a little longer—7 to 12 months—advised beginners to "stay positive and work hard." One had this to stay to nursing students:

> Ask questions. Get as much from your clinical instructor and offer to do more during clinicals. Look for opportunities of exposure to different situations. Start using nursing judgment. Work on your head-to-toe assessments.

It seemed to be common advice among those who've been out of school 7 to 12 months that the new nurse should be patient and try not to feel too overwhelmed at the outset. As one nurse said, "Don't get overwhelmed in the beginning. Everyone has to have a first day of work sometime and everyone has felt that initial anxiety." Another commented, "Patience. The confidence and organization will come with time. For me at 6 months I felt everything fall into place." A third noted, "It's okay to be scared and feel unprepared, but don't be afraid to utilize your resources."

Other nurses emphasized how important it is to ask questions. One nurse said, "Network! Also, don't be afraid to ask questions, and try not to take colleagues' personality quirks to heart." Another said, "Never be afraid to ask questions and keep asking them. No question is ever dumb. Find a mentor you can learn from. If you're given one who is not supportive, ask for new one." One nurse suggested getting the "obligatory" hospital experience initially and then branching off into other areas of nursing. "Research areas of interest within the nursing profession; there are many out there. Get a few years of floor work under your belt, then pursue what you like."

Nurses who had been out of school 13 to 18 months also emphasized the need to ask questions and to ask for help when needed. They also advised "remain[ing] strong and committed." One nurse said, "Be humble, listen to what senior nurses have to say, and don't think your way is the best way." These nurses advised that new graduates "try to think of the big picture not just of a task or result at hand." One nurse offered as an example: "If the patient has crackles [in the lungs], why? Are they on fluids, [do they have a history] of CHF, etc.?" It was interesting that nurses who had been out of school at least 1 year—while also counseling them to ask questions—beseeched new nurses to respect the knowledge of more experienced nurses and to question their own nursing actions instead of merely performing them.

Nurses who had been in nursing 19 to 24 months agreed that it was important to "stay hopeful and be willing to learn every day." They advised that it was important to "learn who you can trust, who really has your best interest at heart, and smile!" One nurse summed it up this way:

> *You have to be open and not guarded. If you are [guarded], you make it difficult for yourself working with others. Listen to them and hear what they are saying. Also, ask questions and clarify answers and orders. This has made me a stronger nurse and a stronger individual in general. People like to know you are listening to them.*

TIPS FOR NEW NURSES

Following is key advice for new nurses:

- *Do not be afraid to ask questions.*
- *Take it one day at a time.*
- *Be willing to learn.*
- *Find a good mentor.*
- *Stay positive.*
- *Be humble.*
- *Listen.*
- *Network.*
- *Remember it is okay to be scared.*

Summary

Clearly, a lengthy orientation of 10 to 12 weeks and a steady preceptor or mentor are vital to a successful transition into the ADN role. It is important that new nurses feel they are safe asking questions and seeking help. New nurses should be told up front that they should expect to feel overwhelmed and be reassured that they can learn to do what is needed.

If students in ADN programs continue to have small patient loads while in school, they need a slow transition when they graduate into assignments of larger patient loads. In addition, they should not be expected to mentor other new nurses in the first 2 years of practice. Most importantly, they should be mentored or precepted by other RNs, and orientation should take place in the setting and on the shift in which they will work.

Educators and those recruiting people to nursing programs and nursing jobs have an obligation to inform prospective students and nurses that the BSN is the desired entry-level degree. It is unfair to promote the ADN or AAS degrees as good options when nurses are being told to increase their level of education. Those with associate degrees expressed the wish that they had gotten BSNs instead. Money and time could be spent on a 4-year degree instead of a 3-year degree and would ultimately increase the benefit to the nurse and the profession.

Chapter 3
The Bachelor's-Prepared Nurse

In 2008, the Health Resources and Services Administration (HRSA) conducted the 2008 National Sample Survey of Registered Nurses. According to the results of the survey, only about half of all RNs have a baccalaureate degree in nursing (BSN) or a graduate degree.

Of course, staying in school long enough to earn a BSN involves higher costs, meaning that nurses with a BSN must work longer to pay off debts incurred. However, the job satisfaction enjoyed by BSN-prepared nurses can make the investment worthwhile (Rambur, McIntosh, Palumbo, & Reinier, 2005). According to a 2005 study by Rambur et al., BSN-prepared nurses experience a higher level of autonomy, a stronger ability to grow as professionals, greater satisfaction with colleagues, and less concern regarding stress and job security than ADN-prepared nurses. BSN-prepared nurses also typically have a higher degree of professionalism (Brooks & Shepherd, 1992; Lawler & Rose, 1987) and are less task oriented than ADN-prepared nurses (Goode et al., 2001).

In a 2009 study of nurses with associate degrees who returned to school after at least 3 years working in nursing, Kalman, Wells, and Gavan found that most of the nurses had always planned to return to school for the BSN. Family factors, however, were a big influence on when they could return. Stagnation and a lack of challenge in nursing jobs also compelled nurses to return for the BSN. To return to school, nurses had to make sacrifices both at home and at work, but they found many personal and professional rewards from achieving the degree.

Background

In response to the 1964 passage of the Comprehensive Nurse Training Act, the American Nurses Association (ANA) published a position paper in 1965 on what nursing education should and should not be (Jacobs, DiMattio, Bishop, & Fields, 1998). Noting the changes taking place in nursing and in health care, the paper recommended that the BSN be required for entry level into nursing. It described nursing education as consisting of the baccalaureate degree for professional nursing and the associate degree for technical nursing. Also mentioned was vocational education for those who planned to work as health care assistants (ANA, 1965; Nelson, 2002).

In 1978, the ANA reaffirmed the decision that the BSN would be the minimal degree required for professional nursing practice by 1985, and that the associate degree was a technical degree. By 1982, several nursing organizations supported the requirement. But by the year 2000, there remained three educational paths for licensure as an RN: associate degree, diploma, and baccalaureate (Nelson, 2002).

Once again, there is a mandate to make the baccalaureate the entry level into nursing by 2020. It remains to be seen, however, if the requirement will be met this time. It is more important than ever to learn how BSN-prepared nurses view their preparation and their experiences as new nurses as we, hopefully, move forward toward this reaffirmed goal.

Preparation

In a 2009 study by Wolff, Pesut, and Regan, researchers asked 150 nurses with varying levels of nursing experience and education about factors that influenced the readiness of new graduates to practice. Here are a few of its findings:

- Both new graduates and nurses involved with new graduates believed nurses with diploma preparation were best able to competently perform in clinical settings.

- Study participants believed that although BSN-prepared nurses received a larger breadth of clinical experiences in school, they were insufficient in depth. Moreover, they believed that the clinical experiences of BSN-prepared nurses did not sufficiently mirror the reality of actual nursing work and workload.

- There was a prevailing view that BSN-prepared nurses were socialized to question more than were nurses educated in traditional programs. Although study participants saw the emphasis on critical thinking in baccalaureate education as important, they perceived it as a potential barrier to competency in technical skills. Even so, they acknowledged that being comfortable asking questions, thinking critically, understanding limitations, and performing holistically were hallmarks of the professional nurse (Wolff, Pesut, & Regan, 2009).

- Study participants questioned the level of commitment of new BSN graduates. They perceived less loyalty among BSN graduates to the unit or organization than to balancing work and home life and to working within a work culture that fit the ideals of the new graduate. Some study participants saw this perceived lack of commitment as justification for not "embracing" the new graduates in the workplace.

- According to study participants, the amount of time required to transition as a professional nurse depended on a variety of factors, including the setting in which a new nurse works and his or her clinical preparation in school. Participants made the point that in traditional ADN and diploma programs, students typically received their clinical training in one facility and therefore were well aware of the organization's policies and procedures. Participants expressed frustration regarding the difficulty in structuring orientation for new graduates in light of the diversity in baccalaureate curricula.

For this book, new nurses were surveyed about how they felt about their preparation to practice as nurses. Many nurses with baccalaureate degrees viewed their preparation as adequate for their new roles. Some nurses said they felt better prepared to practice nursing with the BSN than they had with the ADN. Said one, "This time I was prepared. When I completed my ADN 2 years ago I felt completely underprepared." Another nurse explained the differences:

I've been in the nursing profession for 22 years and have seen many changes taking place in my clinical practice over the years. Going through an accelerated RN to BSN program has enhanced the way in which I practice as well as facilitated my understanding of why change is needed in the nursing profession. The nursing professional standards have been elevated to a higher level, and this has fostered nurses to become more involved in the practice of evidence-based research. Nurses are given opportunities to think "outside the box" and find ways to improve the delivery of care that are safe and cost effective. In these unsettling economic times that we are all faced with, nursing is presented with many challenges. As such, it is essential to stay abreast of new trends as well as collaborate with team members.

Some BSN-prepared nurses are very specific about the ways in which they felt prepared and unprepared. As one nurse put it:

The theory and physiology I was taught during years of school are very useful, as long as I can dig out this information from the back of my mind. It is helpful to be a "fresh" nurse and recall much of this theory through practical patient care. My best preparation overall was a voluntary internship in the emergency department. I learned more practical skills and knowledge during that internship than anywhere. I would encourage any student nurse to take advantage of any additional clinical hours or internships that are available.

I do, however, feel that much of "the loose ends" during nursing school were "caught" by someone else. For example, I have never admitted a patient because another primary nurse was always there to do it. I have never worried too much about checking [a] new doctor's orders because I was relying on either an instructor or another nurse to remind me. All of the little details seem overwhelming now. Prioritization, of course, is the hardest part. When you are a student, you have one or two patients. Then maybe you move up to four or so. But, when you suddenly realize you will need to figure out five or six patients at a time, plus numerous discharges and admits, THAT is something I am not prepared for at all.

Many nurses agreed that their clinical experience while in school was insufficient to meet the demands of the nursing role. "I feel that I was well prepared for the NCLEX (nursing licensing boards) and had a good working knowledge of patho[physiology], medications, and diseases," said one nurse. The same nurse went on to say, however: "I feel that my clinical experience is very lacking." Another responded, "I felt I was lacking clinical skills. I was in an accelerated program, so it was challenging to process all that I was learning and I lacked enough clinical time."

Several nurses said that working as ancillary health care workers helped provide extra clinical experience that enhanced their ability to practice in the new nursing role. One nurse noted:

I feel that we never can get enough clinical experience. The once-a-week clinicals just are not sufficient. I think my experience as a PCT (patient care technician) was a major help in my feeling prepared to begin my nursing career.

Another nurse agreed: "I felt as prepared as I could be [but] I know I had a lot to learn. I think my nursing assistant job and my senior preceptorship prepared me the best."

Several nurses remarked on other aspects of nursing for which they did not feel prepared. One nurse said, "I felt prepared with the basics of nursing but the intricacies of nursing I struggled with." As another nurse put it, "I was prepared to think like a nurse, but I did not acquire the skills I now use on a daily basis."

As with the ADN-prepared nurse (refer to Chapter 1, "The Associate Degree-Prepared Nurse"), prioritizing and managing multiple patients are skills for which many nurses felt unprepared, having cared for very few patients while in school. As one nurse said, "I had some clinical skills needed, such as medication administration, etc. However, as far as prioritizing patient needs and multiple patients, that was a learning curve that took several months."

Interestingly, the need to learn the policies and procedures specific to the organization for which one works was a prevailing concern. Indeed, it was also mentioned in the aforementioned study by Wolff, Pesut, and Regan (2009). One nurse who responded to the survey conducted for this book put it this way: "Yes I do feel that I was prepared; however, there are some skills that you can only acquire once you start at the facility you will work for." Another noted: "I was adequately prepared. I just felt that I needed to adjust to the policies of the workplace that I want to be in."

Regarding preparation, it is interesting to note that the comments of survey respondents who had graduated with their BSN degrees up to 12 months prior were very similar to each other. However, nurses who had been out of school more than 12 months seemed to view their preparation somewhat differently. Among the differences was the awareness of the preparation that is needed to practice in critical care versus in generalist settings. One nurse, who had been out of school 13 to 18 months, said, "I don't think there is much a program can do to prepare a nurse to enter an ICU (intensive care unit). I do, however, feel that I was prepared with knowledge and trained as a critical thinker." Another said, "[I felt] somewhat [prepared]. I did my preceptorship in the ER (emergency room) and I'm employed in medical/surgical/oncology. There's a definite difference. I realize now I needed a lot more clinical practice as a student." Still another agreed: "[I felt] somewhat [prepared]. I definitely had the knowledge, but lacked the hands-on skills for the most simple, daily tasks, like starting IVs and anchoring Foley catheters." One nurse, who had been out of school for 19 to 24 months, summed it up best: "[I felt] somewhat [prepared]; but let's be honest—is there a nursing school ANYWHERE that can prepare you for real life?? 'Real' nursing (after graduation) ate my lunch."

BSN NEW-GRADUATE PREPARATION

BSN new graduates need more preparation with:
- *Prioritizing*
- *Managing multiple patients*
- *Clinical skills*
- *Learning the intricacies of being a nurse*

Nursing Education

In response to the question "What would you change about nursing education to better prepare you for your role as a nurse?" one baccalaureate-prepared nurse answered:

> *Nothing! I appreciate my school's emphasis on evidence-based practice more than I ever did while in school, because I have a sense of independence from my environment. If I have a question about what's the right way to do something, I know that I do not have to accept the advice of a given coworker carte blanche, but*

can do my own homework to figure out my own best practice. I would work harder to be organized during my clinicals and work harder to develop my own system for organizing clinical data.

Happily, several survey respondents remarked that they would change very little if anything about their education and were now able to see what they might have done themselves to enhance their own learning experiences. As one nurse wrote, "I went to an excellent school that prepared me both academically and through simulation. As of yet, I am not sure what I would change about my educational preparation."

Other respondents felt the exact opposite. One nurse shared this perspective:

Being teachable and recognizing that learning doesn't end just because you have a diploma. In general, just not knowing ANY-THING. NOTHING!! I knew nothing!! (Part of this is due to the fact I'm a hands-on learner...even the best nursing program can only allow student nurses so much of that.)

Another said, "I don't think my schoolwork could have really given me the complete view of what it is like to be a nurse. Looking back on it now, I realize which instructors were more based in reality." A third nurse noted:

I don't know if you can be prepared for something like that (being a nurse). You have to experience it and figure out how to deal with it. Maybe a class dedicated to time management and clustering care. You need to be an empathetic person to be a nurse, and to prevent apathy and burnout you need to manage your time wisely at work and especially outside of work—meaning having enough time off to renew, refresh, and appreciate your blessings before returning to work.

Several respondents indicated that they would have benefited from the following:

- Clinical experience
- CNA experience
- Instruction on leadership and management
- Depth of learning
- Higher education

Clinical Experience

When asked how educational preparation should be changed, many respondents echoed the need for more time in clinicals and more realistic clinical experiences while in school. One nurse said, "Putting more value on clinical. We spent most of our time completing care plans rather than working hands on. We should have had more than one patient also." Another agreed, offering these suggestions:

> More clinical hours with smaller student-to-teacher ratio; more time prepping in the clinical simulation labs for practice and exposure; having the semester of nursing students that are ahead speak with the students a semester behind to provide advice and suggestions as well as ask questions.

It is interesting to see that when respondents speak of needing more clinical preparation, they tend to refer to hospital-based nursing. One nurse took this idea further by specifically referring to critical care:

> I would have liked to have a clinical at the end of senior year where I could have done more with the specialty of my choosing rather than less useful courses like community health. I also think critical-care clinicals should be incorporated into every student's curriculum so that one doesn't feel so ill-prepared for the real world of nursing.

NOTE

Anecdotal evidence suggests that undergraduate nursing students do not typically value community health nursing education. They often think that it is not "real" nursing and only value the technical skills they can use in the hospital. This view occurs despite the fact that most actual nursing care takes place outside of hospitals.

CNA Experience

Comments made about the helpfulness of working as nurse's aides or as other types of health care workers were repeated when nurses were asked how nursing education could be improved:

We never got enough practice with IVs. We needed a lot more of that. We also needed more work with the simulation man to practice trauma and code situations. I felt like some information was repeated and some information was skimped upon. I wish we had done some ride-alongs with EMTs (emergency medical technicians) or paramedics. We needed a LOT more practice with medications.

Another said, "I would have liked my instructors to have encouraged working as a CNA (certified nurse's aide) in nursing school because I am learning now without CNA experience it's harder for a new grad to find a job."

I think that there are cogent arguments both for and against advising nursing students to work as CNAs or as other types of health care workers to prepare them for nursing education or while they are in school. Working as a CNA might increase the student's level of comfort with patients and make them more knowledgeable about how a hospital floor or health care organization operates. However, there is a likelihood that the student will begin to see patient care from a CNA perspective, and it is a challenge for nurse educators to change this perspective to that of the professional nurse. Professional nurses should bring theory, research, knowledge of the sciences and liberal arts, and critical thinking to their view of patient care and to decision making. The CNA and other ancillary health care workers are not required to do this to the same degree. As a nurse educator, I can attest that it is more difficult sometimes to acculturate the student with a CNA background to nursing than it is to acculturate someone who is brand new to health care.

Another issue that can be seen from both sides of the coin is the use of simulation in nursing education. One nurse felt that there was too much use of simulation and lab practice and not enough time with real patients:

I wish we had more clinical experience while in school because I feel that too much time was spent in labs and classrooms when the real valued experiences come from the time spent on the floor and with real patients. I also feel that simulation labs tended to just get repetitive and are not always as helpful as the nursing faculty felt they were.

However, anecdotally, I am aware that many students and new graduates feel that their time in the simulation lab was very beneficial and prepared them for patient care.

Leadership and Management

Also mentioned was a desire for more preparation in management and leadership roles. One nurse said, "Maybe having an internship in the managerial position, especially for baccalaureate degree nurses, would be beneficial to help in adjusting to the new role." Others suggested more interactions with patients and with other members of the health care team. As one nurse said, "I would ask to interact more with more of the health care team, such as physicians, PAs (physician assistants), social workers, NPs (nurse practitioners), etc., to better understand their roles." Another nurse put it this way:

> I felt like my education prepared me well. Looking back, I wish more professors [had] asked open-ended questions to the class, especially for us to play to the role of educating a family member. I find I do a lot of education to family members about diseases and medications.

Depth of Learning

One nurse commented that the educational program was great, but that it did not give enough depth in some areas:

> I wish that we were able to delve deeper in some subjects. Yet, while in school, I felt so overwhelmed that I don't think I could have handled any more material. I am lucky; I am a graduate of a great program that was quite comprehensive. Our program also stressed the importance of professional involvement.

"Professional involvement" was not mentioned by the ADN nurses who responded to the survey. Perhaps this is a fundamental difference between the two types of programs. BSN programs, by their nature, tend to emphasize that the nurse is a professional and demonstrate this by encouraging students to read nursing journals and to get involved in nursing education and health policy. One BSN-prepared nurse noted:

> *My involvement in professional organizations helped most when times got difficult for me. I work at the VA (Veterans Administration), and most nurses at my facility are not concerned with what happens in nursing outside their units. I found myself quite frustrated after getting funny looks at work when I mentioned the IOM (Institute of Medicine) report released in 2010, because no one knew what it was, nor did they care. It was comforting to realize that my organizational members also cared—that I was not alone in my hopes for the betterment of the nursing profession.*

Higher Education

Many nurses expressed pride in their colleagues who sought higher education to obtain graduate degrees. As one nurse wrote:

> *I definitely want to get an advanced practice degree. I also finally landed the role (school nurse) where I think that nursing is most valuable. I am now working in a preventative setting instead of acute care. I think that nurses have a huge role to play in preventative care.*

Another nurse expressed that obtaining a graduate degree would help reduce the stress of juggling family and work: "[I am going back to school] because I am not working, and don't plan ever to work again, as a bedside nurse. With more education I feel like I can make a greater difference and have more control over my work-life balance." A third nurse described feeling happy to be a nurse but also expressed a need to move away from bedside nursing:

> *Some days I am happy. I feel hopeful now that I am accepted to the doctoral program. I feel hopeful about my career. If I knew I was going to be a bedside nurse for the rest of my life...I would not be a happy person. I need to know I am in a career that has a ladder to climb. Bedside nursing just is not doing this for me.*

> **NOTE**
>
> *It should be of great concern that new nurses see the pursuit of graduate work as a way to move from the bedside. Why do BSN-prepared nurses not want to be bedside nurses? Does this spring from the hard work they encounter and for which they feel unprepared when they graduate? Or is it due to too much emphasis in nursing school on obtaining a graduate education for the purpose of moving away from direct patient care? Does nursing become a different profession if it does not involve caring for patients but rather involves directing patient care? These are questions that have no definite answers. Even so, they require contemplation and reflection in light of this view of our baccalaureate-prepared new graduates.*

Barriers and Challenges

The challenges include but are not limited to managing time, remembering medications, the technical side of how to prepare a patient before each procedure, and in general remembering what to chart, what to assess, whom to call, and how to assist physicians during each different procedure.

BSN-prepared nurses talked about the barriers encountered as they tried to adjust to their roles as new nurses. Not surprisingly, they were numerous. They included the following:

- Limited employment opportunities
- Making the transition from student to nurse
- Managing one's time
- Lack of professional status
- The learning curve
- The work environment
- Coping with patient illness and unhappiness

NOTE

It is unrealistic to think that nurses can be prepared for every event and detail of nursing work life. However, nurse educators and nurses preparing to graduate can take action to prevent reality shock from such issues as difficulty finding employment (over which nurse educators and students have little to no control), time management, the "good, the bad, and the ugly" of being a nurse, learning common protocols and the business of health care organizations, and how to handle difficult patients.

Limited Employment Opportunities

Similar to ADN-prepared nurses, BSN-prepared nurses reported that finding a job is difficult. As one nurse said:

When I graduated and through taking the NCLEX I feel that I was very prepared, but when I started looking for a job as a new grad I was overwhelmed and felt underqualified. I live in a big city and with hundreds of RN positions posted as available—I still have only managed to get one interview. I graduated with honors and on the dean's list and feel that if hired I would succeed as a nurse but the hardest part is first getting my foot in the door.

Indeed, the newest nurses (those who had graduated between 1 and 3 months prior) identified finding a job as *the* biggest barrier—or, "finding a hospital or clinic that will take a chance and train a new grad." Other nurses echoed this view, such as one who said, "Schools should prepare new grads with a realistic economic view…the job market for new grads unfortunately stinks."

For many new nurses, whether BSN-prepared or ADN-prepared, this difficulty finding a job has been a surprise—in part because many people think of nurses as having multiple options for work. "I thought it was going to be easier to find a career," said one nurse. Another nurse voiced this common concern:

I am starting to get discouraged about the profession. In nursing school they told us nursing was a recession-proof job and that it would be easy to find a career. I am now 3 months into looking and still haven't found anything.

Some nurses described plans to work in certain areas of nursing but ended up working elsewhere—sometimes a positive event and sometimes not. Said one nurse, "My original intention was to work in community health, but I am currently in acute health." Another nurse noted:

Within 8 months of graduating, I had three different jobs. My first two jobs were night shift on a med-surg (medical-surgical) and surgical care floor, respectively. Now that I am a school nurse, I truly feel like I have found my "nursing niche." I finally get to do more of what I love—teach and practice preventative nursing. So, it took a couple of tries, but my expectations finally match.

Transitioning From Student to Nurse

Adapting to the new role of nurse proved challenging for many BSN-prepared nurses, much as it was for ADN-prepared nurses. One new nurse commented:

I am literally a brand-new nurse, so I'm still learning about all of the biggest obstacles...I think prioritization is a huge part. I am also a very organized person, but I feel totally scattered with trying to keep track of multiple patients. I am horrified that I will miss something or skimp on my assessment at the expense of the patient. Also, everything is rushed and that contributes to feeling disorganized and out of control.

Nurses who had been out of school 7 to 12 months agreed. One nurse noted, "Organization and confidence and learning all the new protocols according to [the] hospital" remain barriers. After 1 year as nurses, this was still a concern.

One new nurse described the fear inherent in being the new kid on the block:

> *Being able to ask questions and not being afraid of the more experienced nurses. It is often said that nurses eat their young, which is unfortunately true, and getting over the anxiety of feeling stupid for asking questions is tough.*

Many new nurses found it hard to accept that they were now responsible for the work they did. There was no instructor who would oversee everything they do, covering for them to make sure they do it safely and correctly. Facing the fact that one must act independently and function autonomously was frightening but necessary. One nurse identified "overcoming the transition to becoming an independent clinician" as the biggest challenge. Some nurses were more specific regarding their fears of being expected to know what to do and how to proceed:

> *Calling doctors, and no I am not prepared for this. Also, presenting in multidisciplinary rounds as it is something you are not prepared for during school. You never know what questions might be asked of you.*

Being placed in a managerial role or a position of authority was particularly difficult for new nurses, even with a BSN. As one respondent said, "Adjusting to a managerial position is one of the biggest obstacles in my new role as a charge nurse in the evening shift." Regardless of whether the new nurse was in a supervisory position, learning how the unit or facility works was often an obstacle. Not only did new nurses need to learn where things were, they needed to learn the personalities and quirks of their colleagues and team. As one nurse put it, "I find the technical skills and lack of knowledge about how things flow in the unit are the biggest obstacles."

Time Management

Part of learning about the new environment involves learning how to manage one's time—a barrier often mentioned by ADN nurses, as well. Becoming familiar with documentation systems is also important. One new nurse complained of "time management, organization, and way too much paper work and charting." Another said, "Adjusting to the schedule (rotation days/nights), adjusting to the particulars of the career—the fast-paced environment, learning everything I needed to know to practice safe care, time management."

Although many of the nurses surveyed viewed time management as the biggest challenge after finding a job, most also understood that with experience and time, they would get better at prioritizing and planning. As one nurse bravely stated, "The biggest challenge is time management. I'm up for the challenge." Another nurse had this to say:

TIME MANAGEMENT! ORGANIZATION! Not my strong suits. I do think that these skills are highly tied to personality. I have a right-brained tendency to want to tell a story in general, big-idea terms, and experience the patient in a general sense first (chatting with them, asking questions that I think are relevant when they aren't immediately relevant to their care). I am trying to be more concrete and step-by-step about my workflow and my communication, having a method and a step-by-step plan before I go into the room.

New nurses are taught to be caring, to listen to the patient, to take time to assess patient needs, to hold the patient's hand, and to get to know the patient. In practice, however, nurses must move quickly and complete tasks. New nurses had a hard time reconciling these expectations. As one nurse put it:

Being a competent nurse while being fast while being caring. This can be difficult in emergency nursing. My colleagues want me to be fast and efficient, but I still want to put my caring side to use, too.

Lack of Professional Status

New nurses reported that they were sometimes disappointed that the public image of nursing, the image colleagues have of nurses, and the image nurses have of themselves did not fit with how they now viewed themselves in their new roles. As one nurse wrote:

I think that, unfortunately, nurses are still regarded by the general public as people who hand out pills, fluff pillows, and assist people on and off bedpans…Newer graduates of other medical professions are more accepting of nurses as professionals and colleagues, but society as a whole is not.

Another nurse discussed the lack of value the public and physicians have for nurses:

I see many terrible people graduate who go on to become horrible, frightening nurses; and I meet many wonderful people who fail out. I see nursing consistently undervalued by physicians and feel a temperature change in the public perception of the profession. I feel like what I do is not valued—still very much valuable, but not valued.

Another nurse agreed:

I have always been a healer. I want to help change the problems nursing has. The biggest one is that we are still seen as a helpmate to the physician and not as the first-rate health care professional.

Others worried about the perception their colleagues have of their profession. As one nurse said, "My views on the average nurse have changed. I figured more nurses would care about their profession as a whole rather than only their job." Another nurse noted, "I still believe that nursing has exceptional potential. However, after realizing that not all nurses care about the profession, I am not sure if it will reach the levels I believe it could."

For many new nurses, it was also a shock to realize that not all patients were forgiving or kind to nurses. One nurse observed, "Patients during clinical were usually chosen because they are 'good.' It was a shock to see how difficult people can be." Another said, "I've noticed that I've felt like patients take nurses and health care for granted much more now than when I was in nursing school."

One nurse tried to put this problem in context:

I feel that nursing is a completely undervalued occupation. It's treated like a cost center and you, the nurse, are truly just a resource to the employer. I think that nursing is undervalued just as teaching is and this may have to do with its historic role as a profession for women. It's difficult as a man, especially one that has worked prior to becoming a nurse, to socialize into what feels many times like a subservient role. That said, I can now appreciate how a nursing degree can open up many opportunities beyond the bedside that I would not have imagined while in school.

NOTE

We are very fortunate as a profession to now count many men among our ranks. Unfortunately, the public is slow to recognize men as nurses and their value to our profession.

Another nurse had this to say:

I am realizing more and more how much nurses call the shots and how critical nursing care is to the health outcomes of patients. I feel like there is a huge discrepancy between what nurses do and society's perception of nurses—sometimes it really frustrates me how out of touch society is with the nursing profession.

The Learning Curve

As a new nurse, there is so much to learn—and in most cases, very little time to receive multiple demonstrations or instructions from other nurses. New nurses must be a quick study and catch on rapidly. One nurse put it this way:

The learning curve is overwhelming. It has been difficult to critically think about a situation with such little experience and exposure to such complex patients. It is difficult to keep up with all that I need to do for my patient load.

"Remembering everything, being prepared" are high expectations for the new nurse—and are difficult to meet when one is overwhelmed, having to learn so much so quickly. Despite this, many nurses saw these challenges as positive and part of the steep learning curve nurses must accept:

I face different challenges every day. Sometimes I feel prepared and sometimes I don't. However, I try to step out and meet them head on so I won't consider the same things a challenge next time it happens.

That everyone makes mistakes, and the importance of admitting to and correcting them, can be a hard-won lesson. Indeed, one nurse identified the biggest obstacle to adapting as a new nurse as "learning how to make mistakes." Another nurse, who had been out of school almost 2 years, commented, "You're taught textbook scenarios in nursing school; however, I felt like I learned way more on the job. Nursing school to me is just what it took to be able to take boards."

The Work Environment

Working long shifts and adjusting to the fast pace of the work environment often mean that there is little to no time for nurturing the new graduate. Here was one nurse's experience:

Twelve-hour night shift and a 45–60 minute commute, plus trying to work another job on top of that to help pay student loans. Also, you don't get those "nursing warm-fuzzies" every day on the job.

Another nurse agreed: "Getting used to the 12-hour shifts. Before this, the most I ever worked at one time on a regular basis was 6 hours." Some nurses discussed life as a nurse and the adjustments they had had to make to be able to work. One wrote, "I don't think nursing school completely prepared me for how worn down I would be working night shift." The same nurse continued: "We talked a lot about self-care and the importance of sleeping during the day when working night shift. However, I don't think that my body ever totally adjusted. I know that some people can, but I'm not one of them."

New nurses were also concerned about mastering formal protocols as well as the less-tangible aspects of nursing, such as the culture of the organization. These, however, may be less emphasized in school. One nurse said, "Learning protocol is challenging, but patience allows me to handle the often steep learning curve." Another said, "Socializing and learning the politics of the workplace was the hardest—but I don't know if school can really prepare you for it. It's something that I have learned through trial and error and learning more about myself." Learning how the organization works and how to manage the business end of nursing work is another challenge: "Having to deal with the hospital as a business is frustrating. I can deal with them, but I would rather not."

New nurses must acculturate themselves into the world of nursing. One nurse said that the biggest barrier was "learning how to 'think like a nurse.'" Learning about how colleagues think, how they work, and their work ethic can help new nurses figure out how to cope. One nurse observed, "I had to learn that not all behavior is logical. I also had to learn that there is a minority in nursing that is selfish and does not care who they harm in their misguided pursuit of glory." Another nurse said, "My biggest obstacles to adjustment were not about learning nursing tasks, but about socializing with other health care professionals and learning the politics of the workplace."

Coping With Patient Illness and Unhappiness

Nurses are educated about all kinds of diseases and illnesses that they might see in their patients. They are also aware that it is hard to work with those who are dying and with the bereaved. However, books and lectures cannot possibly prepare the nurse sufficiently to handle these experiences when they first encounter them. As one nurse put it, "Illness, death, unhappiness! Yes, you just have to remember not to take things personally because most times these people are at one of the lowest points in their lives!" Another nurse put this in perspective:

It seems like I learn about three new rare diseases a week, only because my patients have them. I feel prepared for them because nursing school taught me to quickly learn what I need and how to apply it to a patient.

New nurses were faced with the realization that when working with people, such as patients and families, there was no set way to manage every situation. Nursing students often want to have one answer for every case but soon learn that this is not possible. As one new nurse wrote:

I never realized how much time and energy goes into taking care of the family. I work on an inpatient acute unit in a large teaching hospital, and it seems most of my stress comes from the families. I find most of the stress comes from setting boundaries but it is also an intense situation when you help the family cope with loss or grieving.

Facilitators

Similar to ADN-prepared nurses, BSN-prepared nurses seemed to view mentorship as the number-one facilitator. As one brand-new nurse said, "Assigned and unassigned mentors that you can go to for help are amazing. Even mentors from when I was in school that I can still call and ask questions have helped me tremendously." Mentorship can be formal or informal, through a colleague, administrator, or nursing professor with whom the nurse has remained in contact. Said one nurse: "I am still in contact with one of my professors and some professional nurses that are helping me." Another nurse agreed:

I truly would not have transitioned if not for the long-distance support, advice, and encouragement of two of my former nursing instructors. Without them, at this point I believe I'd have no license or even the desire to be in nursing. My start was hard; they buoyed me through and cheer me on still.

One nurse said that "a great preceptor and a unit that works together as a team" were the biggest facilitators. Other nurses sang the praises of long residency programs, such as the nurse who responded, "Year-long perinatal residency...[I'm] hoping extra classes and preceptor time will make the transition more smooth."

It's not enough for the new graduate to simply have a preceptor. That preceptor must be a good teacher, be patient with new graduates, and have an understanding of the need for recent graduates to experience new things even if this causes temporary anxiety. One nurse said, "My preceptors'...willingness to explain everything in detail and their willingness to push me out of my comfort zone have been a huge help." Another nurse agreed:

My preceptor has been very patient with me during orientation and keeps reminding me that it will take me almost a year to begin to feel comfortable in the unit. My supervisor has also been positive, and the rest of the staff are usually willing to help me out or answer any questions I have, even when things are busy.

NOTE

New nurses must be willing to be pushed out of their comfort zone. Not every nurse will be able to cope well with the uncertainty, however.

Other preceptors may not be so patient. As one nurse observed:

My preceptor screamed, "You're all over the place!" on three separate occasions the other day. I find myself distracted by small tasks that other personnel could do, as well as patients' demands that are not critical to their care. It is difficult to focus on finishing one task without letting the next interrupt.

Another nurse said, "The hectic pace throughout the day made it hard to learn, and my preceptor was not always a good resource."

It is important that the new nurse have a consistent preceptor. If there must be more than one, it's important that there be only two, and that they make sure their messages to the new graduate are consistent—not contradictory or repetitive. One nurse noted:

I have had three different preceptors in 2 weeks, and I believe that getting to know each one of them has slowed down my learning (going over the same things I already know three times). Also, the preceptor has a full patient assignment herself—and only gets $40 extra for each day as a preceptor—so that they often jump in and do things before I get the chance.

Clearly, having three preceptors in a 2-week period might confuse new graduates. Another nurse had the opposite perspective, however: "I worked with a preceptor for the first 3 months. I think I would have benefited from working with a few preceptors instead of just one." In this case, perhaps the extended length of time with one preceptor was the barrier. One nurse, who had the "same mentor for 12 weeks," noted that "being with the same person was very adaptive to learning."

Many nurses who had been out of school 4 to 6 months responded that in addition to mentorship, peers and colleagues were important to adapting to their new roles. As one nurse wrote, "Co-workers willing to help. Having a knowledgeable preceptor." Another nurse, who graduated 7 to 12 months before, agreed: "I think it was just a matter of time and trying to learn as much as I could from the nurses around me." Developing and maintaining a support system with other new nurses also seemed to help. One nurse said, "Support from other RNs at my job and maintaining contact with my cohort [were facilitators]." Surveyed nurses responded that support from friends and family was also important. It helped nurses feel valued and that they were not alone.

Ultimately, time and experience in the job helped new nurses feel more secure and confident in the new role. One nurse said, "Performing the usual nursing roles and functions helped me adjust. Experience was my best teacher." Another said, "Time, trial, and error helped me to adjust to this new role." One nurse combined the key elements that facilitate adjustment and saw that one's attitude is also critical: "Just getting in there and doing. Having two nursing faculty/mentors who continued to advise and support me after graduation. Changing my attitude—less arrogance, more humility/teachability."

Summary

As with associate-degree graduates, BSN-prepared nurses discovered that finding a job was not as easy as it had been in the past. And like their associate degree-prepared counterparts, baccalaureate nurses recognized that there are many different types of jobs in nursing, and something can be learned from each of them.

Nurses with baccalaureate degrees—regardless of how long ago they graduated—appeared to largely agree with their associate degree-prepared counterparts on yet another point: that having a good preceptor or mentor (whether formal or informal) and/or a solid orientation were the best facilitators to adapting to the new role.

Chapter 4
Life As a BSN-Prepared Nurse

The previous chapter presented the barriers, challenges, and facilitators baccalaureate-prepared nurses experience as new graduates. These nurse respondents also recommended changes to nursing education as a result of their experiences. This chapter discusses the transition into being a new nurse, the experience of being in a new role, and how the meaning of nursing might have changed for these new nurses since graduating.

Orientation to the Role

BSN-prepared nurses discussed the various ways they were oriented to the nursing role. Some had formal preceptorships, whereas others were assigned mentors. Most had some form of formal orientation. One nurse "received 4 weeks of 'orientation' on the floor with an RN overseeing me." The nurse continued, "After the first week, they stopped providing feedback and viewing my charting even though I specifically stated that I still needed feedback. I learned which nurses to ask for help and which to avoid." Another nurse commented, "I received a 3-day orientation as a charge nurse with the regular nurse on the unit to help me adjust to the new role."

NOTE

Baccalaureate-prepared nurses are trained to be nurse leaders. Managers who foster an understanding of the role and provide orientation to leadership roles are likely to reap the benefits of having nurse leaders who are capable and confident.

For one nurse, the orientation period was particularly helpful:

The director of nursing and other supervisors in the facility I currently work at were very helpful and allowed me to adjust to the new role by giving me orientation as a charge nurse. They told me why I was the best candidate for the position and pointed out my strengths that will help me be the leader in the unit.

Several nurses pointed out that during the orientation period, new nurses must be assertive, ask questions, and try to learn not only what is done, but also why it is done that way. As one nurse wrote:

I am still in the process of nursing orientation, but so far it is going well. There is a certain level of assertiveness that I've needed to practice.... For example, if the mentor does what she has always done as a nurse, I am left in the dark about why or how to do it myself. So, I really try to speak up and say, "Oh, hey, why don't I do that?" "Show me." "Let me do it."

Clearly, orientations vary in length and quality.

I am 2 weeks into my orientation on the general medical unit where I am an RN. I do feel that I was well prepared—but I am anxious about having as many as eight patients at a time. So much of the nursing care I was trained to provide is just not possible with the time constraints of the nurses on my unit. It seems that the nursing process and general assessment skills are most valuable. I'm still struggling to stay organized and give organized reports to the next nurse, among other things.

Orientations seem to range from a day or 2 to 12 weeks and sometimes 1 year in a residency program. But not everyone receives an orientation. When asked whether the new graduate received an orientation or mentorship, one nurse responded, "None, I worked PRN and was expected to hit the ground running." The nurse continued, "A few people offered advice and demonstrated the priorities."

The quality of the orientation, mentor, or preceptor is as important—if not more so—than the length of the time new nurses spend in orientation or with a mentor or preceptor. As one nurse noted:

During orientation my preceptor has been right beside me for the most part and has taken the time to answer questions and wait for return demonstration. Although I am slow, my preceptor has assured me that it is okay, as safety is a priority in training their nurses for quality patient care.

Another agreed:

My preceptors (I have two) allow me to take the lead on one of our two patients at this time while being there for me if I need it. They are very open and eager to teach me and this has made it easy for me to approach them and ask questions.

Interestingly, several nurses had negative things to say about their orientation experiences—even when those experiences spanned several months or combined classroom with precepted experiences. One nurse wrote:

Two weeks in a classroom, going over policies and procedures and practicing skills (such as IV insertion, catheterization), followed by 6 weeks with a preceptor (in my case, multiple preceptors) on my unit. I have not found a mentor yet. There are weekly meetings with the nurse educator, nurse manager, and preceptor to evaluate my performance the week before. I must say, I don't find these cramped meetings that take time out of my preceptors' day to be supportive—I don't like being scrutinized and only the advice of the nurse manager has been helpful.

Another nurse had a similar experience:

I went through a 6-month-long new-graduate orientation. It was developed with the best of intentions but poorly organized. The most beneficial part was meeting people from around the hospital. Now, I know at least one person in most departments around the medical center.

Another nurse with a 6-month orientation stressed the importance of having someone who can teach as a preceptor:

I worked at a magnet facility and started in an ICU. We had six months of orientation that involved classroom and progressively greater and more complex patient loads. The experience was well planned on paper but in reality was sometimes chaotic. The preceptor and the new nurse were not always supported by the other staff. Managers need to know that not every good nurse makes a good preceptor. Teaching styles (or lack thereof) vary immensely and affect the learning of the new nurse.

Several nurses spoke positively about the attempts of their facility to help them with a solid start, such as this new nurse:

For 10 weeks, I worked one on one with a nurse preceptor. I had a max of three: two for days and one for my night shift orientations. The hospital where I work also has a very established new graduate program that lasts for an entire year. Every month, the cohort of new nurses that I started with meet and discuss challenges and other issues we've come up against as new nurses. We also meet to learn more about different resources offered at the hospital.

Another nurse described an in-depth 12-week orientation:

The first few weeks were in the classroom learning policy, procedure, equipment, etc.... Then rotating through various departments within the hospital, a shift on the sister floor of your department, 9 to 10 weeks of orientation in the department you're hired in. During those weeks you are paired with an experienced nurse that you shadow and eventually you'll start taking on a patient load—one to two patients—and end orientation under that nurse being able to take a full patient load—four to six patients....You also complete a packet, filled with competencies and check offs to be completed by you and your preceptor by the end of your orientation.

It seems typical of orientation programs in hospitals to have new graduates experience time on both day and night shifts and sometimes on the evening shift. One nurse said, "I had a 12-week orientation—6 weeks on days and 6 weeks on nights with a one-on-one preceptor." Another said, "I had 4 weeks' orientation on days and 4 weeks on nights. I wasn't too happy with my night preceptor, but I felt compelled to stick it out with her."

As mentioned, having multiple preceptors is sometimes viewed as a good thing—especially if the new nurse has an orientation that spans several months rather than weeks. That being said, multiple preceptors can repeat material the new nurse has already learned or fail to teach material, thinking that others have taught it. One nurse observed, "I had at least six or seven different nurses who oriented me. Some were trained and patient and direct, and others were not trained and harsh and left me alone when I was not sure what I was doing yet."

Communicating With Physicians and Staff

Nurses described their interactions with physicians as mostly positive. As one nurse put it, "It is just another coworker that you must learn to work well with." Nurses who reported having positive experiences working with physicians attributed this to having had opportunities to work with physicians as students. Experience working with colleagues from other disciplines appears to be key to developing a level of comfort with them after graduation. One nurse said:

Yes, I am comfortable working with physicians, because I had clinical at the hospital I work at now and my preceptors helped us with learning how to communicate with physicians. I am very comfortable working with other health professionals from my experience in clinical here and through working as a student nurse at another hospital while still in nursing school.

However, another nurse had the opposite experience:

I have never needed to call a physician yet, and I am afraid to do so. I am trying to observe how other nurses approach physicians/PAs/NPs and how they advocate for their patients. I haven't had much practice yet. I was a CNA before and during nursing school, so I am very comfortable with CNAs. Respiratory therapists are a wonderful resource, as are PTs (physical therapists) and OTs (occupational therapists). It is just going to be a process, to learn who everyone is and questions I can ask them.

For nurses having little experience with the disciplines that nurses typically work with, physicians seemed the most intimidating. One nurse noted:

Most of the physicians in the unit have been very positive with me as a new nurse, and several have volunteered to answer any questions I might have. However, I personally am a bit apprehensive when dealing with physicians, mostly because [of] a lack of confidence and expertise on my part....The lack of experience I have makes me feel less competent in working with other disciplines in the health care team, although I am more comfortable working with them than [with] physicians.

Sometimes, simply giving themselves time to get used to talking and working with physicians and other disciplines reduced feelings of intimidation:

At first it scared me. However, it is now something I appreciate. They often value our opinions and ask for a synopsis from us (as well as the patient) to help them get the full story, which I think is amazing. Absolutely. We each have our own specialties. Let them do what they know how to do and teach me how to help them better care for our patients.

For other nurses surveyed, relations with physicians weren't so rosy. One nurse said, "Their impatience/rushed manner can be intimidating. Might be good for physicians to get a multidisciplinary communication seminar to aid them in better communication skills." Another nurse said, "I'm so incredibly proud of being a nurse, but I've realized nursing is not as respected as it should be (especially by doctors). Physicians and residents tend to demean nursing and do not completely value our input or opinions." One nurse lamented:

I am shocked at how critical I am of physicians—their manner with patients and with nurses....There was miscommunication over the phone, and I ended up crying in front of my instructor and asking her to complete the back and forth with the resident....My challenge is to know enough about my patient to be able to answer their questions. This is nerve-wracking, because I do not have a good grasp of what measurements might be asked about, nor a good memory for values (I need to write everything down, and get faster at finding the important information in the computer).

Differences in shift also played a role in comfort level:

I am growing more comfortable as I gain more experience. Night float docs can be really challenging, but I know they are also overworked and overwhelmed most nights....I feel like I have limited exposure working with other health professionals while on the night shift. There seems to be less coordination of care. I may put in consults, but I don't actually get to interact face to face with many of these professionals.

Typically, as one nurse pointed out, newer physicians "are more accepting of nurses as colleagues than older physicians."

One must not feel intimidated. I feel that it is important to have good working relations with our physicians. As nurses, we spend more time with our patients and their loved ones. This is a collaborative effort, so everyone who is involved in the patient's plan of care is an important facet.

When asked about their treatment by other nurses, BSN-prepared nurses responded favorably in the majority of cases—but not always. One nurse said, "Some were nice and understanding. Others just told me, 'Suck it up and deal; you knew what you were getting into when you went to nursing school.' I also felt like I would never get to day shift being the 'newbie.'" Another nurse said, "My first few weeks were not the most welcoming. I think the staff was not totally sure what I was supposed to be doing or how much I should have known. There was no communication to the unit that I was starting, nor was I introduced to anyone."

Obviously, failure to support new nurses and rushing to judgment about their capabilities do not facilitate their adjustment to the role. As one nurse said, "Some colleagues were very helpful, and some thought my progress was too slow. The ones who were judgmental made me feel inadequate as a nurse even though I'm brand new." Another nurse described feeling like this was a rite of passage:

> I did not feel supported in my environment. There were times I felt hazed and felt like other nurses were not offering any assistance even though they had the ability. On many days, it felt like trial by fire and flying by the seat of my pants.

According to one nurse, the ancillary staff sometimes supports the new nurse more than the nurse's colleagues do: "All of the nurse's aides and managers were extremely supportive and helpful. They were very encouraging throughout my orientation and are still my biggest supporters!" Another nurse spoke to how vastly different experiences can be for the new nurse:

> Techs (technicians) and unit secretaries always were looking out for me and seemed to have my back. Some LPNs (licensed practical nurses) seemed to as well. However, most of the RNs who had been there for years were not very supportive and did all they could to try to drag me down. I had some RNs on the opposite shift that would go to bat for me, though. (That was my first job and for my first year.) I now work at a different hospital, and it is a different story. Everyone supports everyone. Those who are newer than me come to me with questions and for support, and I go to those with more experience than me

for help/support when I need it, even if it's just to bounce ideas around or talk through a situation.

Another nurse lamented that younger nurses were viewed as not having a life outside of work so were therefore expendable:

The older nurses and my manager would say, "You are young; you don't have any family; you can do it!" I hate when they say this to me, because it makes me feel like my life and my time are not as important as theirs. Like there was a hazing problem—even though the nurses I work with are my friends and nice people—it's like they still wanted me to feel the pain and suffer perhaps like they had when they first started working as a nurses.

Sometimes, more experienced nurses may quash the enthusiasm of the new nurse. As one nurse said, "Most think I will eventually realize I can't change anything and focus solely on my unit."

Role Change

As was the case with ADN-prepared nurses, perceptions among BSN-prepared nurses varied significantly with regard to how new nurses' views of the role changed after beginning work in nursing. In most cases, however, there *was* a change—either positively or negatively—from how they had envisioned nursing.

Some were very positive, like this nurse: "In some ways, my new role exceeds my initial expectations of nursing." Another nurse agreed: "My role matches my skills perfectly, and therefore it exceeds my expectation." A third nurse admitted, "I was not totally sure what to expect from my role."

Others were less positive, such as this nurse: "[I work in a] very acute setting, so there is not as much time as I would like to be therapeutic with patients." Another nurse said:

I am not able to offer as much support/direct patient care as I had expected. Too much of my time is spent doing paperwork and not enough with the patients. Protocols and the whims of

*Medicare/Medicaid have far too much influence on my job,
rather than allowing me to meet the individual needs of my
patients as human beings.*

As is probably the case in most other professions, working as a nurse
is different from studying to be a nurse. The real world is bound to be
different from what most people envision when they enter school. As
one nurse said, "The real world is less than the ideals we were taught in
school."

For many new nurses, the realization that there was rarely enough
time to give as much patient care as they would like was a tough one. One
nurse observed, "I've realized how little time is available to spend with
patients to educate them and to get to know them. I'm too busy to be
able to provide truly holistic care, which is disappointing to me." Another
agreed:

*Yes, I see that it is a challenge to practice holism in our current
health system. It's difficult to feel like I have the time to focus
on individual patients when I feel like I have to run around just
to keep up with med pass and charting.*

Some nurses were surprised to find that nursing was much more
difficult than they had envisioned, and that nurses needed to know and do
much more than they previously thought. As one nurse put it:

*I was ready to conquer the world of critical care nursing after
graduation. However, you have to crawl before you walk, and
your first job is only the tip of the iceberg. I need this experience in med/surg as my foundation before I move on to critical
care nursing. Continuing education and reading journal articles
are a must to keep abreast of health care. It's a challenging profession, filled with politics, guidelines, family dynamics, patient
noncompliance, and so much more I had not considered.*

Another nurse said, "This is everything I expected and more. What I
didn't realize was how difficult the first year would be." Some nurses did
not feel the rewards of being a nurse yet outweigh the burdens. As one
nurse wrote:

*My views are conflicted. Although I respect and honor the
choice to work as a bedside nurse, I feel that it is an area of*

employment where nurses are taken advantage of. The pay is good compared to other professions but not great, the hours are terrible, and the workload is relentless. There are many injuries, and many times you feel powerless to affect your environment. There are many other areas for nurses to practice, which makes the profession dynamic despite the challenges of the workplace.

One nurse observed, "I came to nursing as a second career from marketing for the health and beauty industry. I had no idea how hard it is to become a nurse and work as a nurse." Another nurse said, "I have found it to be a much more rigorous field than previously thought." Oddly, one nurse seemed surprised that taking care of the sick was an expectation of the role:

The stress level is extremely high for the entire 12-hour shift. I believe this is a profession where you have to really like caring for the sick and the elderly, because if you don't, this is not a profession [in which] one will last.

Many nurses, however, responded positively about being nurses. They expressed pride in their knowledge and their ability to care for and affect others. Sometimes, new nurses were surprised by the autonomy and trust others placed in them. As one nurse said:

Currently, I feel like my job is much more task oriented than I once imagined. Writing in vitals every 2 hours or turning patients seems to take a lot of time. I also never realized how much autonomy I can really have at times, such as when attending physicians simply ask me what I need. I am really proud to be respected and treated so well, but as a new graduate I am terrified of not knowing enough and not doing well enough.

Sometimes, new nurses saw their expectations and the reality of the role in terms of the big picture. Said one nurse: "I am saving lives, one day at a time. I'm impacting people at their most vulnerable, at their point of need. I went into nursing to make a difference. I am a nurse who IS a difference-maker." After working as nurses, it was not uncommon for recent graduates to develop respect for what nurses do. Said one nurse: "I have more respect for floor nurses. It is a challenging profession— physically, mentally, and emotionally." Another said, "Nurses do much more than I ever knew before and hardly get any credit. It is a stressful and difficult job. It is difficult to care for oneself, one's family, and one's job."

NOTE

New graduates might be better served by their nursing education if they weren't sheltered from the harsh realities of real-life nursing. So much of what new nurses described in their survey responses pertained to the unexpected. New nurses didn't expect the work to be so hard and didn't realize that in certain environments, they would not have time to provide holistic care. Often, they were surprised by the attitudes of physicians and of the public regarding nurses. More shocking were the attitudes of other nurses. Being made aware of these issues while in school might better prepare nurses for work in the field. Educators should offer strategies to help new graduates navigate these rough waters. There should be more practice collaborating with physicians and other health care professionals, taking orders, giving concise and accurate reports, managing paperwork or electronic health records, and learning how the business of health care functions. These are important areas for student learning to ease new nurses' transition to the new role.

The Meaning of Nursing

When asked if the meaning of nursing had changed for them since graduating, recent graduates agreed on many themes. For example, many nurses were pleased to learn that their views of nursing professionals as caring and compassionate were validated. As one nurse stated:

Nursing is the art of providing compassionate care. In addition, learning new ways to deliver care that is safe and cost effective. And finally, being passionate and loving your role as a nurse, in spite of the challenges.

Others expressed that they did not previously have a full appreciation for how caring nurses truly are.

One said, "I still believe that nursing means caring for the patient first." New graduates seemed to have internalized the importance of keeping patients safe and that nurses are often considered the vanguard of patient safety. "I am still idealistic about the role or potential role of the nurse in optimizing patient safety and patient-centered care."

Many were effusive in their pride in being nurses and their love of the profession. One nurse said, "Nursing is more important to me now that I am practicing." Another noted, "I love the profession and take great pride in what I do. I think my pride and love have grown since I graduated and started practicing." Many noted how experience fostered confidence, which contributed to learning to love their chosen profession. As one nurse put it, "The meaning has not changed, but I feel more confident with my nursing abilities." Another nurse said, "The meaning of nursing has not changed. I feel it is a very respectable profession that takes a very caring and empathetic person to truly value a nurse's responsibilities." It was gratifying that new BSN-prepared nurses appreciated what they had been taught. As one nurse said, "Nursing has become much more than a profession. I have learned to love the field in all aspects—research and education included."

It was heartening, too, to discover that many recent graduates have developed an appreciation for what nursing means in the context of health care in general. One nurse put it like this:

In school, my vision of a nurse was an individual filled with compassion and care for the sick, suffering, and vulnerable. Although I still do consider this to be a vital part of nursing, I see another side to nursing that I had not really seen before. Questions such as the cost of health care, motives, and politics within the unit and hospital have suddenly become relevant in my nursing practice so far.

Nurses recognized the importance of nursing to the betterment of health care for all people and could see that what they do as nurses extends far beyond the clinical setting in which they are practicing. One nurse wrote, "After taking a nursing ethics course that touched on the history of the profession, I had a better grasp of the magnitude and importance of nursing to the health care world."

Nurses new to the profession—even those who have not been in the field very long—quickly realized what a difference nurses make in the lives of others. "I appreciate it even more," said one. The nurse continued: "We make a difference in people's lives each and every day." Another said, "It's not just a job; I can help change lives!"

Advice

Recent graduates from baccalaureate nursing programs offered a wide range of advice. Most were enthusiastic and hopeful, encouraging those who follow them to stick with the profession because things do get better. As one nurse said, "Nursing as a profession is tough, but if you are motivated to be a model nurse for others and the people you serve, all the hard work will pay off." Another agreed: "You can do it! It just takes time and willingness to learn!"

A common piece of advice was to ask questions and to admit what you do not know, as pretending that you know something that you do not could jeopardize patient safety.

> Pick a unit where you will feel supported. Don't be embarrassed to ask questions. If you don't get along with your preceptor, have an honest discussion, and you may need to get a new preceptor. Be honest with your preceptor and nurse manager, but not too honest! Remember, you're a compassionate nurse, but you work for a business that needs to make money and will not hesitate to look out for its own self-interests. Always keep your interests front and center.

One nurse put it this way: "Don't be afraid to ask questions, and don't think you are ever stupid; it's not worth killing someone over." Another said, "Be confident, NOT cocky. Always ask questions if you don't understand." A third nurse advised, "Find a good mentor and don't be afraid to ask for help. It's hard and you need to maintain solid social support." One nurse added:

> BE HUMBLE. Do not EVER think you know it all. You don't. You never will know it all. But if you are humble and teachable, your coworkers will teach you, your doctors will trust you, [and] you will make a difference in a hurting person's life every single day.

Another common thread among BSN-prepared nurse respondents pertained to finding employment. One nurse said, "Try to get your foot in a door before you graduate; network." Another noted, "Networking and pounding the pavement are not enough for new grads. There's too many of us, but going on the message boards helps me, as a new grad, from going crazy and going into utter despair."

NOTE

Experienced nurses should not and will not tolerate insolence from nurses who are only just beginning to practice. This goes equally for new nurses who have experience in ancillary roles such as patient care technicians, CNAs, EMTs, and paramedics. They may feel comfortable working with patients, but they must be acculturated into the world of nursing. Those who resist this shift will be looked upon by other nurses with contempt. Those who adopt the attitude that although they have learned a lot, there is still much to learn, will most likely be treated with warmth and appreciation. If the profession is to continue, it needs new blood—especially people who are motivated, willing to learn, and eager to make the profession even better.

Not giving up was a key theme. One nurse said, "Don't get discouraged and keep trying to find that first job." A second noted, "Be prepared to work very hard once you graduate. If you put in the hard work, you will eventually land your dream job. For many new grads, your first position will not be your dream job." Another agreed: "Don't give up with getting that first job. Work PRN or part-time. Take what you can get so that you can start the work experience clock ticking. Then, after about a year, reapply to the job you wanted."

Some offered more practical advice, like this nurse: "Apply for a PCT/tech job in the field you want to pursue. It's the best way to get acquainted to the floor. I did not do this and wished I did." Others were more general: "Expand your horizons. Know your options, and have the heart to pursue what you really want to do."

According to survey respondents, patience is key. One nurse advised, "Be patient. Each day is a challenge, and some are more challenging than others. Find those nurses that are patient and kind and have them take you under their wing." Others were more philosophical: "You will have good days and bad days. Be patient and in the near future you will feel more comfortable in your role as a nurse." One nurse was encouraging: "The first year they say is tough, but never give up and your confidence will grow, I promise." Another agreed: "Just hang in there. It gets better day by day, and it is truly a learning experience. There is not much you can do to prepare for the real nursing role." At the same time, nurses must be positive and flexible, and remain "passionate about learning and caring."

New nurses must make a special effort to learn as much as they can. One nurse put it this way:

> As a new nurse in the workplace, take the opportunity during orientation to learn as much as you can—and keep learning after! Do not hesitate to ask questions or seek help—I have resorted to technicians and the unit secretary to solve problems. Others in the unit who have had years of experience—no matter what position they have—know a lot. See the mistakes you make as a challenge that will build you up as you go from a novice nurse to an expert.

On the subject of learning, many of the nurses surveyed recognized the need to go beyond the BSN. As one said, "I need to continue education to get to the top of my nursing knowledge." Another advised, "Go to graduate school and advance the profession. Tell your friends and family exactly what it is you do—and shine nursing in a positive, professional light."

Perhaps most importantly, those surveyed advised new nurses not to be afraid. One nurse wrote, "Do what scares you, because you never know where it might lead. Take time to reflect upon your experience, and don't be afraid to grow as a person." Another put it this way:

> The best advice anyone ever gave me was, "You are going to suck for your first year." People candy-coat the new-grad experience, but it really is difficult. Someone being honest with me and validating that what I will be facing is what every new nurse faced helped me to feel much better.

In a similar vein, the nurses surveyed were adamant about staying strong in the face of bullying. As one nurse wrote:

Don't let other more experienced nurses bully you, EVER. There is never a time when that is okay. If it is happening, speak up. Confront the person if possible, or if you aren't comfortable, go to a supervisor and voice your concerns. They will deal with it. If they hired you, they want you around; they will help you through it.

ADVICE FOR NEW BSN GRADUATES

Here are some tips for new BSN graduates:
- *Be motivated.*
- *Be humble.*
- *Be patient.*
- *Work hard.*
- *Listen.*
- *Ask questions.*
- *Don't give up!*

Summary

Residencies, preceptors, and a unit that works together as a team are deemed instrumental to a good adjustment. In addition, these nurses—particularly those who had been out of school for at least 4 to 6 months—appreciate the value of their coworkers and peers. One nurse said, "Asking for help, using my colleagues/former peers for support." It is clear that the attitudes of managers and supervisors toward the novice nurse can ease the adjustment and instill confidence.

Being able to ask questions without fear of being thought stupid or incapable is another major facilitator. "Feeling it was okay to ask whatever question I had to an experienced nurse without them getting annoyed [about my] going too slow with progress." Indeed, feeling free to ask questions and reveal foibles—and having colleagues who are receptive to them—is viewed as crucial to new nurses' adjustment to their role. Knowing that it is okay—even important—to ask questions and recognizing that the experience of being a new nurse is not unique to them also helps facilitate the transition for new nurses. On the flip side, new graduates should not convey a cocky, know-it-all attitude.

> *I'm sure I will learn more and more as my nursing orienta-tion continues....So far, my preceptor has been such a useful resource. I am asking millions of questions. I have to keep reminding myself, "This is not about me; this is about the pa-tient." When I repeat that over and over, then it is easier to ask the "stupid" questions. I don't want to compromise a patient because of my insecurity with asking!*

At this point, nurses appreciate that there is so much to learn and there is a need to move beyond one's comfort level to continue to learn and to progress as a nurse. When asked what facilitated the transition, one nurse said, "My preceptors. Their willingness to explain everything in detail and their willingness to push me out of my comfort zone have been a huge help."

Nurses who graduated 7 to 12 months ago also agree that a good preceptor is vital as is a program especially designed to help transition the new graduate. In addition to reliance on the support of coworkers, nurses at this stage are beginning to see the necessity of keeping current clinically and in studying to learn more.

Students and new graduates should be encouraged to ask questions and study hard. Those students who think they can get by in school without studying may pass courses (somehow!), but when they are required to function independently, they will be at a tremendous loss, which will be both embarrassing and potentially dangerous to patients.

Once again, the profession is mandating that the BSN be the minimum degree for entry into practice. It is hoped that supports being put into place to assist ADN and diploma-prepared nurses to achieve the baccalaureate degree will help make this goal a reality. If the BSN truly does become the entry level into practice for all nurses, it will become even more important to standardize what students learn and provide them with increased opportunities for clinical practice in a variety of settings. As we work to improve the quality of baccalaureate education, we should keep in mind the comments and suggestions made by recent graduates from these programs.

Chapter 5
Graduate Programs

Very little literature speaks to the experience of being a new or recent graduate from a master's or doctoral program. In addition, despite repeated and varied attempts, responses to the survey conducted for this book were scant from graduates of doctoral programs. The comments that were received, however, provide impetus for reflection. Because the responses from graduates of master's-degree programs were much more numerous than those from graduates of doctoral programs, those insights will be the primary focus of this chapter.

NOTE

This chapter was based on an informal survey, not a research-based survey. Further research is needed to explore the perceptions of nurses with graduate degrees. For example, it would be helpful to know if it is past nursing experience that truly prepares nurses with graduate degrees to perform their duties in their new roles. Or is it their educational experience? This vital information will help give us an idea of where to go and what to do to produce confident, competent graduates.

Background

Under the auspices of the National League for Nursing (NLN), the National Nursing Accrediting Service issued its first publication outlining the criteria for graduate degrees in nursing in 1949 (NLN, 1977). The 1960s saw a proliferation of master's degrees in nursing, with the intention of endowing nurses with advanced expertise in research, practice, teaching, and administration (Sullivan, Anderson, & Houde, 1983). In the 1970s and 1980s, the literature recognized and discussed the need for master's-prepared nurses with "advanced knowledge and diversely specialized expertise" (Sullivan et al., 1983, p. 344). By 1981, the NLN listed the following as accredited master's degrees in nursing (Sullivan et al., 1983, p. 345):

- Master of science
- Master of science in nursing (MSN)
- Master of nursing
- Master of arts (MA)
- Master of public health
- Master of nursing education
- Specialist in clinical nursing

NOTE

Interestingly, the NLN continues to discuss the need for master's-level education to prepare nurses in specialty roles (http://www.nln.org/newsreleases/masters_r&d_062910.htm). The American Association of Colleges of Nursing (AACN) also recognizes the master's degree as preparing nurses to develop expertise in a specialty area.

Today, the Commission on Collegiate Nursing Education (CCNE) and the NLN accredit more than 300 master's-degree programs and recognize the following master's degrees:

- Master of nursing science
- Master of science

- Master of nursing

- Master of arts with a focus on nursing

The foci within each type of program, however, are varied, reflecting how times have changed in the last several decades. For example, students might focus on nursing informatics or on becoming a clinical nurse leader.

Options for obtaining master's degrees are varied. In addition to the traditional program following the baccalaureate degree, nurses with diplomas or associate degrees in nursing can enter programs that lead to the master's degree. There are also programs that enable people without a degree in nursing to earn a master's degree in nursing. Finally, there are programs that enable students to earn a joint master's degree in nursing with a master's degree in another field (Dracup, 2012).

The literature from the early 1980s suggests that the master's degree was considered a stepping stone to the doctoral degree. Whether it should be considered a reliable barometer of the potential for success in a doctoral program was controversial, however (Sullivan et al., 1983). Spurr (1970) wrote that each degree should be respected in its own right and should not necessarily be considered an indicator of future success in another degree program.

In 1987, Pardue published research that examined decision-making and critical-thinking skills among nurses with varying levels of education. Nurses with baccalaureate and master's degrees scored the highest in critical thinking. No statistically significant differences were found between or among nurses with associate degrees, diplomas, baccalaureate degrees, or master's degrees with regard to how frequently they made decisions, nor in their perceptions regarding the difficulty they had making decisions. However, the study concluded that decision-making was most influenced first by experience and second by knowledge, regardless of educational background.

Around the same time, Cruikshank and Lakin (1986) conducted a study comparing pediatric nurse practitioners (PNPs) with and without master's degrees. They found that work settings and positions differed significantly. Prior to obtaining the PNP, nurses who later earned a master's degree had worked in hospitals and in academe, while those who earned the certificate had primarily been working in nonhospital settings. Nurses were surveyed while undergoing a program that offered both a certificate and a master's degree toward the PNP. By the time of the survey, both groups (master's and certificate) had moved to ambulatory- and primary-care settings. However, more of the nonmaster's-prepared nurses were in nonhospital settings. After receiving their master's degrees, graduates were significantly more likely to be employed in academic settings. Interestingly, the PNPs without master's degrees were more likely to be actually working as NPs than were the master's-prepared nurses.

More of the master's-prepared than nonmaster's-prepared nurses were involved in scholarly activities, whereas more of the latter were taking the PNP certification exam. It is interesting to note from this study that those PNPs who chose to obtain certification but not pursue the master's degree were successfully providing primary care, were practicing in rural areas, and wanted to be valued for their expertise. The authors of the study recommended retaining both options: master's preparation and the certificate to meet the demand for PNPs in rural areas. In addition, they recommended allowing motivated nurses to practice without having to hold a master's degree while freeing up master's-prepared nurses to work in academic settings (Cruickshank & Lakin, 1986).

Since then, additional studies have been done that sought to differentiate the characteristics of those who pursue the master's degree from those who typically do not. One study (Drennan & Hyde, 2008) explored how clinical nurses (clinical nurse managers, clinical educators, staff nurses) and nurse academics compared with regard to which nurses the clinical nurses and nurse academics thought should be selected to pursue the master's degree. Interestingly, clinical nurses supported the master's degree if it served a purpose within the clinical setting but not just for the sake of learning or for one's own growth and development. Fundamentally, the degree must be relevant to their nursing work for it to be supported. This group was also concerned with the psychological readiness and the intellectual ability of some nurses to go on for graduate education.

In contrast, the academics interviewed focused more on the candidate's ability to be successful in obtaining the degree than on the degree needing to serve a particular purpose or position. The academic group did not like having to expend so much energy supporting weak students through graduate programs. In fact, the value of the master's degree has been questioned because of the lowering of standards for admission and graduation. Concerns about this were expressed in the literature as early as 1988 (Glazer) and continue today.

According to Stevenson (2003), nursing has historically not encouraged nurses to pursue a graduate degree until after obtaining some clinical experience. Indeed, this is an ongoing controversy that dates back to at least the 1980s, as evidenced by the aforementioned research. The Nurse Reinvestment Act (2002) permitted loan forgiveness for those who obtained graduate degrees and went on to teach (Allen, 2008). However, many graduate degree-prepared nurses fill academic positions without ever having been taught to be educators and who may or may not have a vast amount of clinical experience (Allen, 2008; Valiga, 2002). Despite support for strategies to increase nursing faculty, a shortage still exists.

There is very little in the literature regarding what nurses do once they have a master's degree or why nurses want to obtain one (Drennan, 2008). Other disciplines have pursued this question and have found reasons that include the following (Drennan, 2008):

- Wanting to enhance career opportunities
- Wanting to enhance earning power
- The desire to learn advanced skills
- The need or wish to change careers

A graduate degree may also be viewed as a way of promoting retention among nurses (Aiken, Clarke, Cheung, Sloane, & Silber, 2003; Drennan, 2008).

Drennan's study (2008), which surveyed graduates from master's-degree programs in Ireland, found that the majority of nurses believed having the degree influenced their subsequent promotions. However, most of the sample was primarily interested in clinical work as opposed to academe or research. Interestingly, the majority had no desire to pursue doctoral education, although those working in academic settings were most likely to consider this an option for the future. The study concluded that the master's degree is not necessarily considered as preliminary to the doctoral degree but as an end in itself. According to Katz (2005), the master's degree should not just be seen as an interim degree or a path for those who cannot achieve a doctoral degree. This is perhaps borne out by the finding that most nurses in the United States who work in higher level clinical positions have master's degrees (Radzyminaki, 2005).

In 2009, Warren and Mills conducted a study to explore organizational incentives that might encourage hospital-based associate degree- or diploma-prepared nurses to pursue a bachelor's or higher degree. Approximately 20% of the nurses in the study had plans to pursue higher education in nursing. This is consistent with the 2008 National Sample Survey of RNs (HRSA, 2008). Those nurses who were content professionally did not see any reason to pursue a higher degree. In contrast, those nurses who were less than content regarding their professional development, income, or work environment were more likely to view a higher degree as a pathway to new and better opportunities. Incentives were ranked according to what would induce a nurse to pursue the bachelor's or higher degree (Warren & Mills, 2009, p. 204):

1. Pay to attend class
2. Classes offered at work site
3. Tuition reimbursement
4. Match work and class hours
5. Paid sabbatical
6. Forgivable loans for service
7. Web-based classes

Researchers observed that nurses who work full time are more likely to be successful in completing advanced degrees if they have mentors, tuition assistance, academic guidance, and tutoring.

More recently, a thought-provoking essay by Donner and Waddell (2011) asks what we should do with nurses now that so many of them are master's-prepared to satisfy them and optimize their usefulness to the profession. Their views are reminiscent of the aforementioned research study (Drennan & Hyde, 2008), which found that clinical nurses felt that the master's degree was justified only if it served a purpose within the clinical setting. Donner and Waddell claim that it is erroneous to assume that every student who embarks on graduate study does so with a specific goal or position in mind. Rather, they posit that many students may expect the graduate program to help them define their professional goals or broaden their opportunities so they can remain or become employed.

This book, in its discussion of the perceptions of associate degree- and baccalaureate degree-prepared new graduates, has repeatedly highlighted the difficulty these nurses have had finding jobs right out of school. In my own experience interviewing prospective graduate students, I have been stymied by the lack of research done by most candidates to learn about the nursing role to which they aspire. Many candidates for the nurse practitioner program could not tell me what a nurse practitioner does (beyond writing prescriptions and "giving orders"), had never shadowed a nurse practitioner, and could not understand why they should be expected to know anything about a program into which they intended to pour a lot of money, time, and effort toward a degree.

Donner and Waddell (2011) postulate that nurses who have no clear idea why they are pursuing a master's degree may end up struggling to fit what they have learned into the workplace and the profession. This, in turn, may affect nurse satisfaction and job retention. Employers, too, may be uncertain about how to utilize these nurses and may place them in positions for which they are unprepared. The authors question whether, as a profession, we give master's-prepared students and graduates the support they need to transition successfully into appropriate roles.

The remainder of this chapter presents and discusses the responses of recent graduates of master's and doctoral degree programs (these respondents had PhDs) in nursing to a survey regarding their perceptions and experiences.

Preparation

For the most part, graduates of master's-degree programs in nursing felt prepared for their roles. However, some mentioned that they could have been better prepared than they were. One nurse said, "I felt prepared to enter the workforce in my new role, not necessarily well prepared."

Another commented, "Not as much as I'd like to have been!" The following comment exemplifies the earlier discussion about whether nurses with master's degrees really fit the jobs they ultimately acquire:

> *Despite my growth and new knowledge, I feel that I need a mentor more now than ever! I didn't realize it at the time, but leadership/management classes would have been helpful (my program was community health nursing). Most of the few jobs out there that require an MSN also require management.*

Others felt that having a lot of experience in nursing gave them the foundation for practice in the new role. One wrote, "Yes [I feel prepared], in that I have been a practicing RN for many years and felt well prepared with the support of my extensive and varied background."

Most respondents began a new role, but a few remained in the role they had prior to obtaining the master's, such as this nurse: "I did not change roles after graduation." It is important to note that a few respondents still had not found jobs even after more than a year out of school, despite being armed with the master's degree. Interestingly, the respondents who had earned doctorates described feeling prepared.

Nursing Education

The nurses who responded to the survey had a lot to say about the nursing education they had received and their recommendations for educators and students. Comments regarding the need to have classes in teaching are typical of those I have heard for years from academic colleagues and with which I agree. It is assumed that because one has a graduate degree, one can teach. However, being a good teacher is a skill and an art. One respondent said, "I would have tried for an increased focus on education—making some of my practicum time focus on in-front teaching."

Interestingly, much like the associate-degree and baccalaureate-degree graduates, some master's-degree graduates expressed the wish that they had had more clinical time. "Less class work, more clinical time." Another nurse remarked, "[I] would require an additional year of clinical training." A nurse midwife put it this way:

First, I would include more home-birth techniques like home-opathy, natural childbirth support, maneuvers, things that help you to rely less on technology and practice, less like a junior doctor (which I think many midwifery schools in this country do now). Also, I would have more focus on clinical education rather than theory. Ours was too heavily rooted in books and busywork the whole program.

Another advanced practice nurse (APN) commented about the emphasis on certain aspects over others:

I would put more emphasis on learning pathophysiology and pharmacology and less emphasis on role definition. I feel that pathophysiology and pharmacology are used in everyday practice and that it's very important to have a depth of knowledge in these aspects. I feel that the role of the NP (nurse practitioner) is so variable between divisions and different regions of the country that it is not only difficult to define the role, but not helpful in everyday practice. Additionally, the role of the NP is evolving as we speak and being defined by the more and more individuals we have entering the work force.

Other nurses commented on the need for more education around finance, business, management, and organizational culture and change. Again, these comments may reflect a lack of understanding on the part of the prospective graduate student when choosing which master's degree to get, or they may reflect the profession's trend of putting out master's-prepared graduates without sufficient consideration of how they might be used, or perhaps both. One nurse remarked that the master's degree "really made no difference. [The] MSN was not necessary."

Some nurses felt their programs were good as is. That said, a faster track to gaining the doctorate was suggested, as was an internship or residency program in the new role. These comments were not unlike those from the associate degree- and baccalaureate-prepared graduates, who voiced a strong desire for these types of programs to better prepare them. Also similar to these undergraduates, master's-prepared nurses asked for good mentors as they progressed toward advanced roles. As one nurse put it, "I would have professors who are MENTORS, ROLE MODELS, and who love what they do."

Surprisingly, a doctorally prepared graduate said that "getting published [was an area for which the nurse did not feel well-educated]. This is one area that my PhD did not really focus on." This is quite shocking, as doctorally prepared graduates are typically expected to publish. More investigation needs to be done with doctorally prepared graduates, especially in light of the doctorate of nursing practice (DNP), to see if this omission is pervasive.

NEEDS FOR NURSING EDUCATION

According to the nurses surveyed, the following are key needs for nursing education:

- *More clinical and science-based education*
- *Education courses*
- *Mentors*
- *Role models*
- *More education in finance, business, and management*
- *More education about organizational culture and change*
- *More emphasis on publication and research*

RELATIONSHIPS WITH FACULTY AND COLLEAGUES

The survey conducted for this book asked recent nurse graduates with master's or doctoral degrees about their relationships with faculty and colleagues while in school. Only this group was asked this question, because students at the graduate level are often considered more like peers and colleagues to faculty than are undergraduate students. Overall, the experiences were positive. One nurse answered, "While they were my professors, I felt more like colleagues than in my undergrad or even in my first master's program." Another nurse said, "Spectacular. We are one community, and we share our expertise as colleagues. We utilize each other's strengths and assist each other with our challenges."

However, nurses who had been in distance education or online programs felt closer to their fellow students than they did to professors. As one nurse wrote, "Distant with faculty (online), but close with classmates." Another said, "Distant, but I was in a program that facilitated distance students. The faculty felt to be more distant than the students."

Many developed relationships with their peers that they had come to value. One nurse wrote, "Very collegial—lifelong friends and networks were made. We were not competitive; we worked to get everyone through the process." Another said, "Amazingly, in a distance program, I was very close to my colleagues. I could not have made it through without them and their support."

Some nurses observed that while some faculty were good, others were not. Said one nurse, "I had some good faculty and some not-so-great faculty." Another agreed: "Some [were] good, some not so good. [It was] really based on the educator and their [desire] to facilitate learning." Perhaps this is to be expected in any program.

One nurse observed that professors did not always give students credit for their previous nursing experience or knowledge: "The biggest problem was dealing with...professors at the university who were always making sure that the experienced nurses didn't think that they may have actually brought some real nursing knowledge and experience with them to grad school."

Doctorally prepared nurse graduates, however, were generally positive about their relationships with faculty. One wrote, "Faculty—respectful of their knowledge and willingness to guide me in the journey. Grateful for one amazing chair/mentor."

Barriers and Challenges

Nurses with a graduate degree faced many of the same obstacles as other levels of nurses. Here are a few examples:

- **Limited employment opportunities.** Although some of the nurses surveyed saw having a master's degree as increasing one's marketability, others had not yet found jobs. One wrote, "Biggest obstacle: Currently, a difficult market to be in a new position postgraduation." Another agreed: "Finding a job is the biggest [barrier]. Every job requires recent exp[erience]!" One nurse educator put it this way: "I'm afraid I will forget some of what I learned about teaching and research by the time I find a position."

JOB OPPORTUNITIES FOR NURSES WITH ADVANCED DEGREES

The survey asked this group of nurses whether their job opportunities had increased due to their graduate degree. Some said yes. As one wrote, "Absolutely! I can go almost anywhere I choose and feel prepared to step in." Another acknowledged, "My first master's was as a CNM; this degree was for FNP. So my opportunities are more because my field of study was much broader." Interestingly, however, most said no. As one nurse put it, "No! Quite the opposite! All the employers in the area seem to want experienced NPs only." Indeed, for many nurses, having a nurse practitioner certificate seemed key to getting a job. Others were not so sure they would not have had more job prospects as an RN. One nurse observed:

> *I suppose I have more opportunities, although RN positions in this area are present. I feel like the APN opportunities include much more "intellectual" work and more liability with less support from colleagues and from the nursing board, [the] practice act. There are still "gray areas" and not a lot known by administrators about my role and by MDs about what I can do, etc. I don't have those ambiguous expectations in my RN role.*

Often, those who felt limited were in specialties, such as the nurse midwives who wrote, "Yes and no. More opportunities to practice as a practitioner in different settings, but in the state I live in there is only one hospital regionally that allows midwives to practice in the hospital. So you are limited on where you can work to do births." Another said, "As a registered nurse, technically I could've worked anywhere. In reality, all I knew was women's health. So, as a CNM, I don't think that my job prospects increased, but I do have a job." One nurse educator had a similar concern: "Not really. [I] cannot land a job in nursing education with my MSN, despite working on a postmaster's certificate in nursing education."

Many spoke of the continuing lack of understanding about what NPs do, hampering their ability to obtain a job. Although it's true that through the tireless efforts of nurses and others, NPs have gained more notoriety in the US, and that patients and physicians seem much more aware and appreciative of what NPs and APNs offer, this response indicates that more work must be done in this area.

- **The work environment.** For any nurse who moves into a new position, regardless of education, becoming familiar with a new organization and its policies and procedures is difficult. One nurse explained, "For me, [it was] the change from one company to another and adjustments needed in policies and procedures." Another responded that an obstacle was "learning to understand organizational proclivities."

- **The learning curve.** All levels of graduates seemed very concerned with all that they were expected to know and be able to do. One nurse wrote, "Keeping abreast of current research, keeping up collegial interactions with MDs, not making errors, anticipating challenging patients' needs, learning to take time off—I am not quite prepared for them." Adding to the burden of recently graduated nurses was concern about meeting and exceeding patient expectations for care—or, as one nurse put it, "being able to find the time in each day to go above and beyond each patient's expectations." As one nurse put it, "The main challenge that I face is regarding learning and diagnosing the overwhelming amount of different syndromes, etc. It's very challenging to put together all the information and see the big picture." Another described the biggest challenge as, "Competence. Luckily, I feel comfortable asking questions, but I know a lot of new grads are not, and this could be a major hindrance to their knowledge and patient safety."

- **Time management.** How to best manage one's time and balance one's life worried nurse graduates at all levels. As one nurse wrote, "My biggest challenge is balancing work and life. I hope I'm prepared to face the challenge—I'm still working on it." This was true even of those nurses with advanced degrees—although one would think that by this time, these nurses would know how to prioritize their work and manage their time. Perhaps their inability to do this effectively is due to some master's-prepared graduates moving into high-level nursing roles without ever having worked as RNs.

- **The perceptions of colleagues and peers.** As one nurse put it, "Feeling insecure, feeling like [I] will be a failure or injure/harm a patient, worrying about colleagues' perceptions and treatment of me."

NOTE

Interestingly, the observation that "nurses eat their young" was pervasive, and applied even to this level of nurses. This is especially curious considering that many nurses with graduate degrees come from nursing backgrounds and are not new to the culture of nursing. It seems that the profession is hard on anyone who is new to a role within nursing, regardless of how long a person has been in the profession or how well-educated he or she is.

In addition to these barriers—which were common among many of the nurses surveyed, regardless of level—new nurses with graduate degrees noted a few that were unique to them:

- Adjusting to a leadership role

- Lack of business background

- Getting published

Adjusting to a Leadership Role

Not only were these nurses expected to be experts on the clinical front, but they were also expected to act as leaders. One nurse described this as the "expectation of dual roles of leadership and direct patient care provider." These dual expectations, placed on these nurses simply by virtue of their having an advanced degree, placed some new graduates in a tenuous position for which many were insufficiently prepared. As one nurse wrote:

> *It was a new role for me to be in a position of authority and leadership. I found this transition difficult when I started in my current position as a CNM (certified nurse midwife) in an office where I am the youngest person, yet I am "in charge" of people who have been there for years and who are much older than I.*

Another nurse described it like this: "Transitioning between a staff nurse where I carried out the orders and looked to other people for the answers to the person giving the orders and having other people look to me for the answers." A third wrote:

> *It is really difficult to "flip the switch." I am now delivering babies where I was a labor and delivery nurse. My former coworkers have been supportive, but I find [it] difficult to "give orders." I end up doing a lot of things myself that a lot of other providers would not do.*

For some, the difficulties lay in having to learn a new role from scratch, something one nurse described as "horrible." The nurse continued, "[I] went from being an expert to a novice all over again. Not [a] fun feeling, like you don't know what you are doing."

This transition may be especially difficult for nurses who have stayed on at their places of employment but are now in a new role that might threaten others. "It's hard in nursing to move up," said one nurse. That same nurse continued: "Peer RNs are not very supportive of becoming a midwife." Another nurse said, "I still worked as an RN while waiting for my NP job. Peers on the unit always asked me about the progress, taking boards, where I was going, making jokes, etc., which gets tiring."

In addition, new roles added new types of pressure—what one nurse described as "different constraints on my time and pressure to conform to a medical model." Many of these nurses worried about "obtaining and maintaining a credible position with the staff," not to mention "litigation in the US [and] being on my own after only 1 year of clinicals."

There seemed to be a common thread to how these nurses described their challenges. One can even sense a hint of anger in their responses, such as this one:

Moving from bedside nursing to provider, taking on that role. The reason I feel mostly able to make this change is based on my own strengths and experiences. If it depended on the absolute bashing of students and any confidence they may have had in themselves or their practice, I would be in serious trouble.

Recent master's-prepared graduates were also challenged by their new, more independent role. One wrote, "Independent decision making—[I] don't feel at all prepared for this!" Another said, "Big role change, functioning and thinking independently." Other challenges included finding resources to fulfill their responsibilities and, as one nurse wrote, "multitasking in many areas that I had only read about/done assignments on previously."

On the whole, nurses described a less-than-smooth transition into new roles. Sometimes, the problem was simply the growing pains of being in charge when before, there were others to fall back on. For some, however, this was not difficult. One nurse wrote, "I was ready to move into a new role, so it wasn't too difficult. The experiences I had on the unit prepared me for dealing with people in the new role." Other nurses spoke about the new role as challenging but rewarding. One wrote, "For me, it was not difficult in that I have always had challenging roles as an RN, I am always eager to learn/stretch, and I have been ready for this for a long time." One nurse observed that "Shifting from direct patient care to administrative responsibilities has clarified my professional goals. I was not prepared for this aspect of moving into a role as educator." Another nurse mentioned "new expectations, roles, and responsibilities. I am interested in stepping away from the bedside and [starting to make] positive changes to patient care from a system level." A third nurse was very positive about the result of obtaining a graduate education: "I have expanded my thinking from bedside nursing to system-level nursing."

Lack of Business Background

Although nurses who had recently graduated from undergraduate programs did not generally view their lack of business knowledge as a barrier, many master's-prepared graduates did. One put it this way:

I got zero preparation for the business part of practice. I knew billing and coding were crucial—but now I am hypervigilant because it's my paycheck (and the success of the practice). Just wish I had learned this stuff in school.

Another nurse commented, "[It's an] entirely different focus— on finance rather than hands-on clinical, but clinical background is imperative."

Getting Published

For the doctorally prepared graduates who responded to the survey, having to publish—but no longer having faculty support—was the biggest challenge. One nurse wrote, "Not being in school anymore. Having to publish."

The survey conducted for this book asked this group of nurses whether they had been mentored to write for publication or conduct research. Overwhelmingly, their response was no. Moreover, few expressed a desire or interest in doing so. However, one doctorally prepared nurse noted that although she did not feel prepared to write for publication, "I am working with a research mentor to assist me in the publication area. I sought out such a mentor."

A WORD ON PUBLISHING AND RESEARCH

The responses to these questions are confounding, to say the least. As a nurse educator and clinician, I have strived throughout my career to teach and mentor others to write and conduct research. In every program in which I have taught, my colleagues and I have encouraged students to pursue research and publication—even in colleges or universities where faculty members were not as successful in these areas as they would have liked to be.

continues

Those in academe are constantly reminded of the importance of research and publication but are insulated from how other nurses, regardless of educational level, view these aspects of the professional role. Perhaps because many master's-prepared nurses work in clinical settings and are removed from academe, they are not encouraged to engage in scholarly activities after graduation. Even so, one would assume that graduate-prepared nurses would receive encouragement and instruction on how to perform research and to write while in their educational programs.

On the first point, while I fully support integration of evidence-based practice (EBP) into research classes, I have noticed that some programs fit in this EBP content at the expense of students conducting research studies or developing proposals. Must we sacrifice one for the other? In my view, all graduate degree-prepared (if not baccalaureate-prepared) nurses should understand the value of research and possess at least the rudiments of how to design and conduct a research study.

As for the second point, in my work as an educator and an editorial board member for various journals, I have observed that on the whole, nurses do not write well. Moreover, nurse educators are often reluctant to push students to write well, arguing that nurses don't need this skill in the clinical setting because they use abbreviated notes in charts or checklists in electronic health records. The best way to learn to write is to read. Nurses with graduate degrees should read widely and be knowledgeable in areas outside of nursing, so that they convey an image of a well-educated professional. If we want nursing to be recognized as a profession comprised of people who think critically and are valued for their minds, it behooves us to make the ability to write fairly well a prerequisite of entering a graduate program and the ability to write very well a mandate to graduate. Nurse educators should encourage students to read widely and to develop interest and knowledge in a variety of subjects. After all, professionals in other disciplines tend to write well and to be able to speak intelligently about many things. The public often forms opinions about people who cannot do so as being less professional or well-educated.

Of course, writing for publication is another matter altogether. Even nurses who write well must be taught this skill. A mentor can help nurses understand how to measure up to the

> *requirements of journal editors and book publishers. Those who move into postdoctoral programs tend to receive formal mentorship to conduct research and publish. However, not all graduates from doctoral programs can afford—in terms of time or money—to continue on in a postdoctoral program. This makes it difficult for them to publish. If we are to continue to advance the profession, however, graduates of doctoral programs should publish. But perhaps the only way for these graduates to learn how to publish, and to conduct meaningful research, is to arrange more formal mentorship programs for those graduates who do not plan to continue on in a postdoctoral program. It is worth considering having nurse leaders, published academics, and researchers mentor all new doctoral graduates for a limited period.*

Facilitators

Much like their associate-degree and baccalaureate-degree counterparts, recent graduates of master's-degree programs highlighted mentors and a solid support system as the most significant facilitators to transitioning. Here are a few of the comments they made:

- "Nurses who are willing to be leaders and help new nurses."

- "Talking to those already in the role, finding support, supportive family."

- "Great coworkers, support from all levels of the organization, and my years of nursing experience."

- "Prayer; a supportive family; reminding myself to provide safe, not perfect care; advocating for myself to get a transition period."

- "Talking with other APNs."

- "Coworkers and [the] development of patience with myself."

Orientation

For nurses with advanced degrees, experiences varied markedly with regard to the length and type of orientation received. One nurse enjoyed 4 months of orientation: "[I had] 4 months working directly with an

MD (medical doctor) while waiting to be credentialed, seeing patients, developing treatment plans and follow-up needs. [I] also had suture and radiology training." Another received minimal orientation but spoke of having a preceptor:

> I have had little orientation whatsoever, because I was a student in the same facility. That being said, my preceptor (now my partner) has been wonderful to me. She is very generous, patient, and understanding. I have precepted new nurses and know how difficult that process can be.

One nurse said, "[I had] minimal orientation to [the] first job from a preceptor [except for] paperwork; [for the] second job, [I had a] 2-week orientation, then seeing patients; [I am] feeling unsure." Another graduate had an "8-day preceptorship." A third respondent was fortunate to have a residency:

> I had a 13-week residency period; I asked for a modified appointment template to begin with after the initial period; I sought out experienced colleagues who were happily willing to mentor me, in addition to consulting my assigned advisors.

Most respondents did have a mentor—something viewed as particularly positive in helping to transition doctorally prepared graduates. In their case, they derived benefit from a variety of mentors. One nurse responded as follows:

> I do not have a mentor at my job; however, I do have an exceptional mentor at school. She provided a great deal of assistance in helping me find my way in nursing. She also provided job opportunities and training for potential leadership roles in nursing.

One nurse, however, had no mentor and was left to arrange her own meetings: "I sought people who had experience in nonprofit organizations and took them to lunch to gain insight. [I] also fostered relationships and maintained them through email."

One midwife wrote, "I was/am mentored mainly by my assistant chief and chief. The other midwives and physicians I work with have been very supportive as well." In contrast, another midwife lamented, "[I did] 10 births before being on [my] own. That's not that many."

Communicating With Physicians and Staff

As one might expect, this group of nurse graduates felt more comfortable overall with physicians and staff than did their undergraduate counterparts. In many cases, this was likely due to having experience as nurses. Other factors likely included their greater understanding of the culture of nursing and how physicians and staff interact within and outside of that culture.

NOTE

Many nursing programs now enable students with no experience in nursing to obtain graduate degrees in the field. One wonders whether those graduates have the same level of comfort with physicians and staff. Unfortunately, the survey did not differentiate these nurse graduates, so we do not know the answer.

One nurse graduate, however, seemed angry about her experience with staff and administration:

I've experienced a lot of resistance from a variety of directions. Support staff, organizational peers, and even my boss, who seem threatened by the development of my role. I would recommend transitioning into a position where there are others doing a similar job.

Another master's-prepared graduate had this to say about the relationship with physicians: "I still feel the power distance between myself and certain physicians but [am] overall comfortable, depending on the individual." Regarding the relationship with staff, the same graduate noted: "I feel like those who have many more years of experience look down on me, discredit me." Another nurse said:

Some colleagues felt I was getting special treatment compared to their initial adjustment period; others felt I was doing well but suffer from lack of self-confidence; others try to push me to assume more administrative duties.

The transition was particularly difficult for master's-prepared nurses who continue to work in the same facility as their student practica or where they previously worked as RNs. Often, other nurses and staff had trouble seeing the nurse in a new authoritative or autonomous role, with the ability to make decisions. As one nurse observed, "I have begun practicing where I was a student and for the most part have had a lot of support from staff. I have found that occasionally I do have to prove myself to the nurses." Other nurses also noted this need to "prove" themselves, with some feeling the need to stand up for themselves. As one nurse wrote:

> I think some tried to take advantage. At first I was not confident enough to stand up for myself and was finding myself doing the roles and job duties that the MAs (medical assistants) and other support staff should be doing. Over time, I learned to assert myself better.

However, another nurse had the opposite experience:

> Feedback is consistently positive. I knew and was known by all my colleagues and supervisors from my last clinical rotation [that] was here, and it was already documented that I was coming in with a solid skill set.

Many viewed this level of graduate as being able to jump right into a role and fulfill it as an expert by virtue of having a graduate degree or being in a higher position. Sometimes, the expectations of the master's-prepared new graduate were higher than they could fulfill. One nurse observed, "Most were understanding, but [I] feel like they expected more than I was capable of doing well." Another wrote, "It's a very hard first year—they are supportive, but you are also expected to know more than you do." The fact is, these nurses require orientation and mentoring in their new roles just as anyone else does in a new position with new responsibilities.

Like new associate- and baccalaureate-level graduates, new graduates with advanced degrees experienced some antagonism from their coworkers. One nurse observed, "Supervisors were supportive, but all colleagues had different attitudes towards new nurses." Perhaps these coworkers felt threatened. As one nurse wrote, "They were resistant and seemed threatened by advanced education." Or maybe these coworkers were anxious to show that their knowledge and experience trumped a nurse with a graduate degree. Indeed, in some cases, they might have been right to think so. Many new graduates with advanced degrees have never worked as nurses, have worked as nurses only for a limited time, or worked in entirely different areas than those for which their graduate degrees prepared them.

NOTE

It is unfair for new graduates to think they know more than an RN who has been practicing for a long time. It is equally unfair for experienced RNs to think their RN experience translates to areas in which the master's-prepared nurse should be especially knowledgeable, such as leadership, systems theory, administration, finance, quality improvement, and so on.

Overall, however, nurses felt that their reception was positive. One said, "They feel that I have a great deal of potential working as a nurse leader." Another wrote, "[They are] very open and willing to let me make mistakes and ask lots of questions." A third agreed: "Very supportive with open communication and were willing to make adjustments as needed." As one nurse put it, "I am lucky to be in a place that is very supportive; many of my fellow graduates have not had that same experience." Another tempered her response: "I am acting/working in the role of a provider versus a nurse and it feels much better at work. However, the battle for respect as a profession that is mainly women continues everywhere else."

Unlike their associate- and baccalaureate-prepared counterparts, nurses with advanced degrees were asked specifically about their relationships with administrators once they assumed their new role. Most were quite positive, noting that the relationships were collegial. They felt respected and supported by their administrators.

Role Change

The survey asked recent graduates whether their perceptions of what their roles would be had changed since assuming those new roles. Overall, nurses with advanced degrees responded that their new roles were what they had expected them to be. Some, however, said that they did not yet know, while others admitted they had not yet found a job. One nurse wrote, "Unfortunately, I do not have a new role at this time. I am currently seeking a new role that will match my expectation."

The concerns that were expressed revolved mostly around being less involved in patient care than expected. One nurse observed, "It is what I expected a med[ication] management position to be, [but] less impact on the patient than I hoped." Another nurse described feeling isolated: "No, it is much [harder and more] isolated than I imagined." Perhaps this was an example of the old adage, "It's lonely at the top." Still another lamented, "The hours are even longer than I ever thought they would be." One doctorally prepared graduate, however, had positive things to say, noting that she now felt "more supportive, inclusive, and holistic in my approach. [I] use evidence to assist in decision making."

The Meaning of Nursing

Respondents were fairly equally divided with regard to whether the meaning of nursing had changed for them since graduating with an advanced degree. Many commented that it had not changed. As one nurse wrote, "The meaning of nursing hasn't changed for me. It has only been strengthened. I have discovered in my role as a CNM why patients seek midwifery care versus medical care. We are nurses—we listen to them and spend time with them."

Others' views changed significantly. One nurse observed, "I have a greater sense of what nursing is all about—respect, compassion, and dignity." Another agreed: "It truly is a service-oriented calling; very selfless." A third nurse noted, "I have a more global view of the impact of what we learn/teach."

For some nurses, the change in their view of nursing was less general. One nurse said, "Now I am a medication prescriber and not a staff nurse so yes, nursing, or looking at the patient holistically, has changed from their basic needs to their needs by body systems." Another noted, "[It's] more about patient advocacy than technical skill."

Advice

Interestingly, the advice given by nurses with advanced degrees closely mirrored that given by associate-degree and baccalaureate-degree graduates to their peers. As one nurse said: "Have confidence in what you know and what you don't. Ask questions when you don't know the answer."

Like their ADN and BSN counterparts, nurses with advanced degrees emphasized the importance of mentors and preceptors. One nurse wrote, "Look for mentors before you need them." Another said, "Get as much experience and learning from your...preceptor [as possible]." A third, who started by saying, "Move slowly, [it] takes time," agreed: "Rely on coworkers, experience, and mentorship." One doctorally prepared graduate looked at mentorship from the other side of the coin:

We need to be supportive of our new grads across the board—at all levels. We need to mentor those coming behind us. We need to change the old ideas, which can be difficult, as they seem to hold the power!

Other nurses with advanced degrees focused on how nurses should *be*. One wrote, "Be engaging and actively pursue your passion." Another said, "Be strong and assertive." Yet another wrote, "Remain curious, willing to stretch and grow, and leave your preconceived notions at the door! This is an exciting time to be an APRN, and most boundaries are self-imposed."

Some nurses offered more practical advice—much of it pertaining to obtaining additional schooling. One wrote, "Really investigate institutions and find the right fit. Graduate school is doable—even while working, even with a family—and it is worth it!" Another noted, "Do it while you are still single and before having children; advocate for yourself, no one else will." A third nurse urged, "Do not stop for long at the completions of earned degrees," but another disagreed: "Take one day at a time and realize that some things need to be put off for a later time." Another nurse suggested, "Get all the clinical hours you can." With regard to work, one nurse advised, "Know the expectations of the division that you are hired into and keep an open line of communication."

Summary

Much can be gleaned from what recent graduates of master's-degree and doctoral-degree programs tell us about their experiences—although not much of it is new. In some cases, the profession is clearly aware of the issues and is already trying to address them, such as how to best prepare nurses for employment once they graduate. Other issues have been controversial for some time, such as which jobs should require a graduate education, what the standard should be for achieving a graduate degree, and whether the MSN is merely a stepping stone to a doctoral degree or is valuable in its own right. It is doubtful that the profession will resolve them for a long time, if ever.

One critical issue is our rush to get new nurses out into the field. This causes us to push people into master's-degree programs and, now, the DNP before they have gained any nursing experience. Although many nurse leaders contend that this has not hurt the profession—indeed, it may be helping in some ways—this practice does create its share of problems. For example, nurses with a graduate degree but without nursing experience are often pigeonholed into a specialty, without ever having the opportunity to see what they might like in nursing—a profession with so much to offer. Nor do they gain an understanding of the culture of nursing or the nitty-gritty daily aspects, such as communicating with physicians, prioritizing one's work, and working with patients and families.

Given that we seem to be encouraging people to obtain master's degrees without truly understanding what they are getting themselves into—not to mention the fact that we have more graduates of master's-degree programs than we now know what to do with—perhaps we should rethink this aspect of nursing education. Ideally, we should encourage people to have a specific idea of what they intend to do with their degree when they graduate. Prospective master's-degree candidates should research the role in which they are interested, shadow someone in that role, and be able to articulate what they hope to do when they assume that role. The time and effort spent conducting this research will not be wasted; indeed, it may save time and effort in the long run when the new graduate is looking for a job. Students spend a lot of money, as well as time, in school, and nursing programs at every level are strenuous and intense. Before taking on what can be the most rewarding and inspiring work in the world, students should make sure they are suited to it—and that it is suited to *them*.

If we fail to implement these suggestions, then perhaps these advanced degrees should be general degrees. Indeed, I advocate requiring a master's degree or a DNP for entry level to match several other professions. Those nurses who earn them should not be given first jobs beyond their capabilities. Alternatively, we need to provide them with much more clinical education in school, as well as cover other areas of the profession in which they may be lacking—for example, business, finance, organizational culture, and change. (The updated *Master's Essentials* [AACN, 2011] delineates the expectation for these graduates to know more about business-related topics.) In addition, those nurses we educate to fill the nursing faculty gap should be trained to be educators. Neglecting to give them the skills they need to be great teachers does a tremendous disservice to them and to their students.

Nurse educators should appreciate the experience that graduate students with a background in nursing bring to the academic environment as they usher them into a world in which leadership, high-level clinical skills, and scholarship are the expectations. Students who can relate what they are being taught to previous experience are more likely to retain new learning. These students should feel like colleagues. For my part, I have always learned from my graduate students. They have come from a variety of nursing backgrounds, and their experiences have enriched class discussions.

Like their undergraduate counterparts, master's-prepared graduates need mentors. The profession has come a long way in formalizing mentor and preceptor experiences, particularly for BSN graduates. Graduates with master's degrees need this as well. Indeed, for these graduates, it should be taken even a step further; they should be formally mentored with regard to scholarly activities so they learn how to apply what they learn about research and writing to their new roles.

Speaking of writing, all nursing curricula should place much more emphasis on writing well. It is an enormous error to underemphasize the role that this skill plays in how others view nurses. Furthermore, respected professionals READ. Nurses with graduate degrees embarrass the profession when they are not well-rounded and do not present the image of someone who is aware of or concerned with the world around them. An educated person should not only be knowledgeable in the area in which they work, but they also should convey the image that they have read widely and are aware of other cultures and beliefs. Master's-prepared graduates should also be taught how to manage their time in their new roles, which may require more precise and higher level time-management skills. In addition, they should be taught how to work autonomously and independently, as well as how to connect with colleagues so they have a solid support system. It's critical for new nurses with graduate degrees to take steps to avoid feeling isolated when they are no longer peers of the RNs with whom they used to associate.

If possible, nurses who graduate with a master's degree should try to find a job in a setting in which they have not previously worked or been a student. Often, it is difficult for others to see them in their new role—although this may be less difficult for APN graduates who were students in a private practice or clinic before they practiced in the advanced role. Even still, providers who precepted them may need time to trust them and treat them as autonomous providers.

Chapter 6
The Chasm in Nursing

I once conducted a qualitative research study of elder nurses to discover how they thought the profession had evolved and the kinds of changes they had seen or experienced. This sample of nurses first helped me realize that there was a definite gap between bedside nurses and academic nurses. They described nursing in days long past, when *esprit de corps* (their words)—nurturing new nurses and taking pride in being an RN—was key to the profession. They were shocked to observe as older nurses (and, later, as patients and spouses of patients) that this *esprit de corps* no longer seemed to exist. These nurses came from a variety of educational backgrounds and experiences in nursing, but they all noted that there was divisiveness in nursing that had not been there before.

In contrast to that earlier study, which focused on nurses who had long been in the profession, this book presented the views and concerns of people who had only recently become nurses or obtained a graduate degree in nursing. As you learned, there were many similarities in their perceptions and experiences—especially among associate degree-prepared and baccalaureate-prepared nurses. Indeed, it seemed some experiences of the brand-new nurse transcended level of education. One interesting difference, however, was that although many associate-degree nurses saw the value of continuing on for a baccalaureate degree, they did not seem to have the same distaste for bedside nursing as that expressed by several of the baccalaureate-prepared nurses. Somehow, baccalaureate-prepared nurses had gotten the idea that one must move away from bedside nursing as soon as possible. Indeed, the profession seems to consider moving away from the beside to be a point of pride. (Note that for the purposes of this chapter, "bedside" refers to any direct patient care.)

It appears that this attitude is contributing to a growing lack of unity within the nursing profession—the divisiveness those older nurses had observed. The fact is, there is a widening chasm between nurses who provide direct patient care and those who have no contact with patients at all, even though both groups consider themselves to be nurses and would be horrified to be thought of as otherwise. Indeed, it would be difficult to find another profession in which there is such a large gap.

Unfortunately, in my experience, nurses who opt to remain in direct patient care rather than pursue graduate degrees seem to be looked down upon by nurses who *do* have graduate degrees. In addition, although many nurses who have advanced degrees still provide direct patient care, nurses who do not interact with patients directly sometimes look down on the nurses who do. Indeed, they seem to espouse the view that all RNs should go beyond the baccalaureate degree to a graduate degree specifically to move away from the bedside. At the same time, those nurses in direct patient care appear to have little respect for nurses in academe or research who do not also maintain clinical practice. They seem to think—perhaps justifiably so—that nurses who do not maintain some level of clinical practice cannot know what it means to take care of patients, and therefore may not be able to educate new nurses using up-to-date information or conduct research that is directly applicable to clinical practice.

A WORD ON NURSING RESEARCH

It is all well and good for nurses in academe to dictate how others should think about nursing and provide theories regarding what nurses should do, but it is only fair for nurses in the trenches to question how realistic and pragmatic some of these ideas really are in practice. As a researcher and a scholar, I believe that researchers who design studies that have direct impact on patient care or the work life of the nurse are contributing to the profession. However, many studies are done that have no obvious relationship to improving patient care or nursing work. Unfortunately, if the researcher who proposes a study hails from a Research I institution, chances are high he or

> *she will receive funding for that study—regardless of whether it has obvious clinical value. And even with studies that do have obvious clinical value, the people who most need to know the results are unlikely to have access to the information because they will not read the journal in which the results are published or attend the conference at which the work is presented. (More on these problems later in this chapter.) In the end, the study will simply join the long list of works that do not serve to improve the profession or the work we do in any way. Even so, academics, researchers, and theorists will pat themselves on the back and tell each other how much they have accomplished for nursing.*

There seems to be a point in every nurse's career when the nurse is expected to go on for higher education or to move to a role that may involve patient care but that is not directly at the bedside. It is difficult to pinpoint when this is, and it may vary for each nurse, but in my experience, the expectation is there regardless.

For nurses to be educated—intentionally or not—that bedside nursing is somehow beneath the professional nurse is to completely devalue what nursing *is*. It is unconscionable that people within our own profession would seek to devalue who we are, separating nurses into those who "get dirty" caring for patients from those engaged in other activities that, theoretically, support them. Those who support nurses who provide direct patient care are typically in academe or research, but these categories are not black and white. Many nurses who teach or conduct research continue their clinical work, and many nurses who provide direct care to patients engage in teaching and/or research. However, as mentioned, there appears to be a fairly distinct line in the sand between those who provide direct care at the RN level and those who work primarily in academic settings.

Aren't we all nurses? Isn't our first responsibility the welfare of patients and patient care? Why should nurses who remain in bedside nursing, regardless of the venue, be made to feel they are not ambitious or motivated to better themselves, or that they lack the intelligence to get a graduate degree and do something else? Aren't all nurses prepared to make important and lasting contributions, regardless of whether they stay in direct patient care or they leave it for "scholarly" activities? Shouldn't nurses respect what each of them brings to the profession and not denigrate others simply because they are pursuing an area of nursing that we have not chosen ourselves?

Perhaps it is because we have varying levels of entry into practice that there is insufficient respect for one another. A nurse with a BSN may not be able to appreciate what an ADN-prepared nurse knows. The nurse with a master's or doctoral degree may not remember how much they had to learn to become a nurse. In addition, the nurses who obtain master's degrees without ever having worked as nurses may have little to no understanding of what it is like to work as a generalist nurse and consequently little appreciation for what these nurses know. Regardless of the reason, we should stop looking down our noses at one another and honor our colleagues.

What Is Nursing?

All this begs the question, what is nursing, really? Although attempts have been made to define nursing and to unify the profession with one overarching philosophy, they have not been successful. Yes, nursing is replete with theorists who try to make sense of what nursing is and proscribe what nursing should be or how nurses should define themselves. But it is difficult to put one's finger on exactly what the ideal nurse should do or be.

Besides, do we want to be so proscriptive about what nurses must do to *really* be nurses? In 1860, Florence Nightingale wrote of what nursing is and is not, but most of what she wrote pertained to direct patient care. Does that mean any nurse not directly involved with patients is not really a nurse or is not really doing nursing? Nursing itself has expanded since becoming a profession, with nurses found in many more settings than ever before. If we attempt to delineate what a nurse is and what a nurse is not, we may exclude people in nursing roles that, while perhaps not traditional, remain useful and important.

NURSING'S IDENTITY CRISIS

In recent years, the nursing profession has experienced an identity crisis of sorts. Ever since nurses moved away from starched white uniforms, stockings, and shoes in an attempt to garner public recognition of nursing as a profession, patients have become increasingly unsure about just how to differentiate registered nurses from other staff. (As but one example, consider that many patients automatically assume that male nurses are physicians by virtue of their gender.) It is as if we were trying to blend in rather than stand out among other health care professionals and paraprofessionals. Unfortunately, in our attempts to identify ourselves as being on par with other professions, we have moved away from what singularly identified us—at least outwardly— as nurses: the uniform.

If patients cannot identify us, how are they to know that we are the thinkers? That we are the ones who not only carry out orders, but also use critical thinking to analyze what is best for them? That we are the ones who question when necessary because we know our patients best? The ones on the front lines of advocacy?

Over the years, many older nurses have told me that the very reason they became nurses was because they admired an early role model—maybe their mother, maybe a neighbor, maybe a friend—who looked so proud and professional going to work in their whites. This is not to suggest that we should go back to that. However, the profession must recognize the need for the public to identify who, among all the health care professionals and paraprofessionals they may encounter in a health care setting, is the registered nurse. Fortunately, many facilities and agencies are taking great pains, such as ensuring that the letters "RN" are clearly visible on nurses' scrubs, to remedy the confusion patients have regarding who, exactly, is the nurse—and many have been successful.

The Chasm in Academia

During the course of my career, I have worked at a medium-sized state university and a large-sized state university—one in a rural setting and one in an urban setting. I have also taught at an Ivy League school, at a small private Catholic college, and at a nonreligious private university. The nursing departments at all of these schools included both graduate and undergraduate programs except one, which had only a graduate program.

The faculty at each school comprised master's-prepared and doctorally prepared nurses, and included researchers, clinicians, and the rare few who were both.

Incredibly, none of these schools was consistent in how they taught nursing, at either the undergraduate or graduate levels. For example, at one university, a dean told me that pathophysiology was not relevant to practicing nurses. The dean believed that nurses need not know why they are caring for someone in a particular way; they just need to know how to care for them. (The same dean also told me that research was not relevant to learning pathophysiology.) At another university, however, the faculty decided that even graduate students who would not be using their master's degrees in strictly clinical roles should learn advanced pathophysiology (along with pharmacology and health assessment) because as graduate-prepared nurses, they should have an advanced level of clinical knowledge.

NOTE

Continuing education requirements are another good example of the variations in nursing education. For example, consider health assessment. Although the findings can make a significant impact on the plan of care, many nurses in clinical practice have lost their skills in this area and examine patients incorrectly. It might seem unthinkable that a nurse could continue to practice clinically without regularly demonstrating current knowledge and expertise, but states vary widely on whether to require continuing education for nurses. And even among those states that do require continuing education, there are variations in how many continuing education credits should be required to maintain an RN license.

Nor were these schools consistent in their expectations of faculty scholarship or faculty practice. In some of these schools, I was considered a paragon for my scholarly and clinical achievements. In others, my work was considered insufficient—and there was scant interest in my clinical background. Incredibly, a research study I submitted while teaching at a state institution received no recognition until I started working at the Ivy League university. This begs the question as to whether it is the reputation of the university or the merit of the research that matters most. One wonders how much good work is being lost to the profession when the researcher does not have the bona fides or is not associated with a prominent university to receive a prestigious grant.

Some institutions whose primary focus is research make a pretense of caring about how their students are educated to be nurses. Their main focus is acquiring research funding and in publishing good research. Interestingly, it is often the schools with the fewest resources that do the best job educating nurses, because their primary focus is on teaching. I value research, and I admire most of the work done at high-level research institutions. However, their work is often at the expense of good nursing education. These schools of nursing should demonstrate their commitment to education by recruiting and retaining faculty who are good teachers and by providing the resources needed to show that nursing education is at least as much of a priority as research. Conversely, those schools of nursing that do not make research or scholarship a priority along with nursing education should work to alter their environment to fully support both. My point is that all nursing graduates should receive the highest standard of education and should be taught by faculty who role-model the importance of research and scholarship, regardless of the school from which they graduate.

The faculty role also varied significantly among the nursing schools where I worked. For example, in most cases, the nursing faculty shared in the governance of both the school of nursing and the university itself. Faculty members were empowered to suggest and make changes. At one university, however, the nursing faculty had minimal influence in governance. Committees were organized to give the *impression* of faculty governance, but in actuality, a hierarchy of administrators—who could choose whether or not to consider faculty opinion—made the decisions.

Why are there so many differences among schools of nursing? I think this has to do with how nursing faculty and administrators perceive themselves and their responsibility to nursing education. However, those of us who choose to be nurse educators, whether or not we are researchers, should be consistent in the priority we place on nursing education. We should have a reasonable expectation that all nurse educators will engage in some level of research and scholarship, maintain currency in clinical practice, and be passionate about teaching. To do all of this means that schools of nursing must structure classes to allow faculty to have time for clinical practice and time for scholarship. The way things are currently structured makes this nearly impossible. Many faculty members must work outside of normal business hours to do either or both. Nursing faculty members typically carry heavy teaching loads. If we appreciate how vital it is for faculty to engage in practice and scholarship and to role-model that to students, we can work toward restructuring nursing education to allow time to pursue these activities. Other service-oriented professions are confronted with a similar dilemma. Perhaps we can learn from them regarding how they integrate scholarship, teaching, and practice.

NURSING: A CALLING?

Although the expectations for student learning seem to vary widely among nursing schools, what these schools do have in common is the increasing tendency to "spoon feed" students. Regardless of how stringent (or not) the admission requirements or how high (or low) the board scores, students are given multiple chances to succeed—even when it is clear that they do not appear to have the calling or even the ability to be nurses. This begs the question, is nursing a calling? Or is it merely a job? Clearly, this is an issue that nurses have debated for some time. I think the answer is different for each of us.

For many nurses, regardless of whether they are on duty, whether they are still working or retired, they are "always a nurse." The minute someone realizes you are a nurse, you become the go-to person for all sorts of health- and illness-related questions. Even if they want to, nurses cannot escape this. For nurses with substantial clinical experience, this becomes ingrained—a part of who he or she is, for better or for worse.

This is not to suggest, however, that all nurses are angels of mercy, always empathetic, or even good at being nurses. As in every profession, there are nurses who view the job as just a job and cannot be bothered when they are off duty. The point is that regardless of how we view ourselves, the public sees us as nurses all of the time. Therefore, we must be conscious of how we appear to the public.

Most nurses would seem to agree that regardless of whether nursing is a calling or merely a job, it takes certain characteristics to be good at it, most importantly intelligence and a passion for helping others. Some may say that is cliché, but if one is not passionate about helping others, he or she is less likely to put forth the tremendous effort it takes to learn how to be a competent caregiver and advocate. Intelligence and academic ability are vital, because nursing is so heavily science-based. Nurses should be well rounded and inquisitive, because that means that they take an interest in the world around them and are likely to be lifelong learners. These qualities combine to convey a professional image. So, let's not take just anyone into nursing. Let us be more circumspect in whom we choose to join our ranks, because they will represent all of us.

The Chasm in Professional Journals

The myriad answers to the question "What is nursing?"—and the chasm illuminated by those varying answers—are reflected in the different types of nursing-oriented journals and magazines.

Case in point: Recently, I brought a variety of nursing journals to my graduate research classes and asked the graduate nursing students— all of whom were RNs—to evaluate them. I wanted them to determine whether each journal included research (and if so, at what level, and the complexity and detail with which it was described), who the authors were and their credentials, and the intended audience and focus of each of the journals. With respect to the latter, I encouraged my students to consider whether these coincided with whether or not research was presented.

In general, they found there were two types of journals: clinical journals and research journals. The clinical journals were either focused on a particular specialty or provided general clinical information. Most were geared toward RNs with entry-level RN education; these generally featured articles written by nurses with bachelor's degrees. A few, however, were aimed at advanced practice nurses. The latter—which included articles written by nurses with master's degrees and, occasionally, doctoral degrees—tended to include more evidence-based information with some research. Although there were one or two articles that were theory-based, none of the clinical journals relied on theoretical frameworks. The articles in the basic clinical nursing journals often included anecdotal experiences of nurses in clinical situations. Advertisements tended to focus on clinical jobs, uniforms, and stethoscopes.

> **NOTE**
>
> *Clearly, academic or research nurses, especially if not in clinical practice, may find the journals targeted toward RNs with an entry-level education to be uninteresting. Alternatively, they may find them incomprehensible, as these articles assume a certain level of clinical expertise and/or experience, which academic or research nurses may or may not have.*

In contrast, the research journals featured articles whose authors had research doctorates and were heavily theory-based. These journals, which contained advertisements for academic faculty, were clearly targeted to graduate degree-prepared nurses. Although several of the articles in these research journals covered clinical topics and research questions, the graduate students who read them expressed confusion about what the articles were trying to say. While it is true that these students were new to graduate school and had yet to complete a graduate research class, they were *not* new to nursing; even still, they were largely unable to make sense of the research articles that were intended to improve clinical practice. It is unlikely that nurses with associate degrees or diplomas would be able to use this information, either.

For many research studies, it is sometimes difficult even for those with advanced degrees to determine how the information gleaned from each study might be applied to improve the quality of patient care or the work-life experiences of nurses. This might explain why, when reading research journals that covered studies that presumably had application to clinical practice, the graduate students—experienced RNs—could not explain how they could apply much of the information. But how is it useful to spend a lot of money and time doing research ostensibly for the benefit of the bedside nurse if the bedside nurse does not understand the information or how to use it?

Needless to say, these nursing students were surprised by the sheer variety of journals and the myriad ways in which information was presented. They were similarly shocked to learn that there was such a disparity among nursing-related journals.

So what does all this say about the ever-widening gap in nursing? It might indicate that although nursing is considered a single profession, we are not unified in how we develop its knowledge base; in our clinical, academic, or research expertise; or in how we think of what nursing is and is not.

> **NOTE**
>
> *In my own experience, I often found that what served as a laudable scholarly contribution to the literature and research in one institution was barely noticed in another. Sometimes, this was because the journal in which the research was published was viewed as too clinical. Other times, it was because the information had not been disseminated to a national audience. The fact that the information was distributed through publication and presentations to nurses who could directly apply the information to patient care was viewed as unimportant. I took this to mean that those nurses were not considered to be of significance, as they were unlikely to read high-level research journals and most likely could not afford to attend—and even if they could, would feel very out of place at—research conferences.*

The Chasm in Nursing Organizations and Societies

As with nursing journals, the nursing profession is replete with organizations and societies that clearly gear themselves toward certain spheres within nursing. Some of these societies require demonstrated academic success to join; others charge steep membership and induction fees. Once again, certain segments of nurses seem to be intentionally excluded. Although numerous bedside nurses have performed countless important services for patients and families, these organizations do not laud their accomplishments, because they may not have graduate degrees, do not publish, do not conduct research, and cannot afford high membership fees. Simply being a good nurse should be enough to garner such recognition.

Moreover, the nursing organizations currently in existence are terribly fragmented. It is no wonder, then, that despite the existence of 3 million nurses in the US alone, nursing still suffers from an inability to harness its strength to accomplish more as a profession. Even organizations that recruit members from all areas of nursing often make it expensive or inconvenient to become a member. The traditional struggles continue and are perhaps getting worse by the increased fragmentation within the profession. How then are others to view us as professionals?

The Chasm in Professional Conferences

Professional conferences are another area in which the chasm exists. Indeed, some research conferences—and the nursing societies that sponsor them—seem to intentionally exclude nonresearchers by making the fees for both faculty and students exorbitant. Many nurses work at academic institutions that offer only scant funding for professional-development activities, and nurses who work at clinical institutions simply cannot afford to attend these conferences. The same issue also prevents undergraduate and graduate nursing students, who could greatly benefit from attending professional conferences, from participating. As a result, the conference attendees—along with the society members—tend to be comprised of elite groups who work for high-level academic institutions. This is another example of how much of the scholarly work that is done never reaches those who could use it to improve patient care or the work life of nurses, because they have little to no access to it.

A large segment of RNs and students who could contribute other points of view is left in the cold. When only high-level researchers and academics participate in these conferences, it engenders a skewed view of what it is like in the real world of nursing. The further removed these nurses become from the real world of nursing, the less they can contribute in any meaningful way. Sure, they might make themselves feel good about what they do, but are nurses who are in the position of translating this work into improvements in patient care even aware of it? All RNs—whether they are engaged solely in direct patient care or are working in other areas of nursing—should be enthusiastically encouraged and empowered to participate with academic nurses (and vice versa) in activities that have the potential to advance the profession.

A WORD ON "NURSE LEADERS"

Interestingly, the average bedside nurse has rarely heard of those whom the profession calls "nurse leaders"—that relatively small group of nurses (many of whom have not been involved in patient care for years or even decades) who have published books and articles in prestigious journals and/or have been busily working with large research grants. Given the fact that often, the average nurse has never heard of or read about them (unless they go on to graduate school or join certain professional organizations), it is worth questioning how much influence these "nurse leaders" actually have on the profession. Although this elite group may attempt to perpetuate the notion that the profession needs them, it is hard to see how their contributions have directly improved patient care or the work lives of nurses. Rather, their disconnectedness from the "average" nurse may have contributed to the chasm in nursing. They may be somewhat responsible for creating these elite societies, conferences, and journals that justify their own place in nursing but ignore the mass population of nurses in the field.

In spite of this, many nurses who do go on to graduate school are encouraged to emulate these nurse leaders by publishing and conducting research studies. The message, however, is clear: One cannot progress to be among these elite "nurse leaders" and maintain a clinical practice. Perhaps if this message were changed, and nurses were encouraged to maintain a clinical practice while pursuing research and publication, their work would be more relevant to bedside nurses. Also, if everyone had the same educational foundation, and if nursing organizations and conferences were accessible to all nurses, then the bedside nurses would know who their leaders were and could learn from them. They could thus apply the wonderful work that is being done in the academic and research worlds to their clinical practice, and researchers would have a more realistic idea of what they can do to actually support nurses in the field.

> **NOTE**
>
> *The literature now speaks of translational research (Feldman, 2008)—that is, the effort to make research meaningful in the clinical setting. This is great in theory, but if the profession still suffers from a great divide, it will have little long-term success.*

Bridging the Chasm

When defining a "good nurse," many describe a clinical nurse as one who has good assessment skills and sound judgment, is intelligent, and can function independently, but who also knows how to work well with other disciplines. If that definition is correct, how can one call a nurse who does not take care of patients a "good nurse"? Can a researcher whose work has no impact on patient care be called a good nurse? Can an educator who does not practice clinically be called a good nurse?

There are no easy answers, but these questions further illustrate the chasm that exists between the bedside nurse and the nonbedside nurse. This chasm must be bridged at least to some degree so nursing does not fall completely asunder. Fortunately, there are a number of ways to bridge this chasm, while still retaining what is great about the advances that have been made in nursing scholarship and professional practice.

The most crucial of these is to finally set an entry level to practice. Although the doctorate of nursing practice (DNP) was developed to be an entry level into practice for the nurse practitioner, it makes more sense for the DNP—which gives the graduate a practice doctorate—to be the entry level into basic nursing practice. Like the BSN, the DNP should be standardized with certain required courses that prepare the student for entry-level practice as a nurse. However, unlike the BSN, the DNP could be a 5-year degree that also includes extensive preparation in research and scholarship. This will level the playing field but set a higher standard than the current fragmented programs.

With a DNP (or something similar) for all RN preparation, there will be a heightened appreciation for both the clinical and scholarly aspects of nursing. Other health care disciplines such as physical therapy have made a practice doctorate the entry level into practice. If everyone had a DNP, it would be difficult for anyone to think of nursing as anything less than a profession; all nurses would be trained to read and understand research, and no one could feel belittled or undervalued. We would continue to have research doctorates that would educate nurses to be researchers, but all nurses would be prepared to read, understand, and apply research. Perhaps, we would not then require the MSN degree.

I have previously written about my research on registered nurses with disabilities (Neal-Boylan, 2012). I proposed that we admit students for their intellectual capability and not exclude anyone because of physical impairments. Clinical experiences could be structured to prepare nurses with disabilities to go into areas of nursing that utilize their ability to think critically and do not rely on physical ability. If the DNP were to be the entry-level degree, it would support tailoring clinical experiences for all students (with or without disabilities), even while didactic content would remain the same for everyone. Students with an interest in pursuing an advanced practice degree could then take an additional year to obtain a certificate in their specialty area.

NOTE

While on the topic of education, let me add that it might be best to defer teaching of nursing theory until the student has completed entry-level education. Often, students in undergraduate programs are so wrapped up in learning to perform the skills required in nursing, they are unable to make more than a minimal effort in their theory classes. Consequently, they do not understand or use theory in their nursing practice. In contrast, when graduate students are taught theory, they have some frame of reference— especially if they have already had some nursing experience. Indeed, my graduate students love talking about how using nursing theories could help them be better nurses. They even learned to develop their own theories of nursing and found that they could implement those theories when at the bedside. Many nurse educators think nursing and borrowed theories are not necessary in nursing education. I disagree. A well-educated professional should know and understand the theories that buttress practice, but the nurse need not learn them until they have the wherewithal to apply them.

In addition to standardizing nursing education at a higher level, nursing organizations must unite forces and should no longer be driven by making money. (It is true that membership dues are necessary to run an organization, but making them affordable will result in *all* nurses feeling welcome. This will in turn cause a spike in memberships, and the coffers will fill.) Instead, the emphasis should be on what nursing is supposed to be. Conferences should focus on information that is evidence- and research-based but that can be directly applied to caring for patients or improving the work lives of nurses. Similarly, nursing journals should offer information to the RN that is both general and specific, so that all nurses can stay abreast of the latest clinical and research developments. Separate journals for advanced practice might remain specialized, as they often focus on the diagnosis and treatment of specific groups of patients.

If all nurses were educated in the same way, belonged to the same organizations, and read the same journals, not only would this unify the profession and add credibility to what all nurses know and do, but also nurses would be more likely to maintain a higher level of clinical skill and knowledge. Nurses who read journals and attend conferences that discuss a wide variety of topics that are clinically applicable are less likely to forget important clinical skills such as health assessment. Yes, specialty journals and organizations have value, but not if they serve to further divide nurses or limit access to important clinical or research knowledge.

Moreover, nurses who no longer care (or never cared) about clinical practice should no longer teach in nursing schools, regardless of whether the school focuses on undergraduates, graduates, or both. This particularly applies to nurse educators who teach courses about patient care. If we are to teach students the current standards of care, then we should be actively engaged in caring for the types of patients about whom we are teaching. A nurse who loses (or never has) a clinical interest cannot truly be dedicated to improving patient care and belongs in a nonclinical profession. To be a nurse is to have a clinical focus, regardless of clinical setting. It is not fair to students, either, to be taught by people who are not current clinically. Nurses who teach courses about patient care should be required to maintain a faculty practice to keep current with the profession and provide up-to-date information to students. "Faculty practice" has been broadly and variably defined. Sometimes it is so broadly defined that it is hard to discern how it informs clinical expertise. Faculty practice must inform what one is teaching so that what is passed on to students is current and relevant.

DIMINISHING THE CHASM

There are things we can all do to help diminish the chasm between the bedside nurse and the academic nurse.

- *Value the bedside nurse.*
- *Value the academic nurse.*
- *Be an academic nurse who is current clinically.*

  or

  Be a clinical nurse who is current with research and professional issues.
- *Make nursing organizations affordable.*
- *Combine some organizations so that those that remain have large memberships with which to effect change.*
- *Make nursing conferences affordable and applicable to clinical and academic nurses.*

Most of all, academic nurses, researchers, and theorists should not look down their noses at nurses in the trenches, who do the *really* important work of nursing. After all, it is these nurses in the trenches who make what the academic nurses do possible. Indeed, were it not for nurses at the bedside, ivory-tower nurses would have nothing to research or to write about. As such, they should respect what bedside nurses do and their right to remain at the bedside.

In turn, bedside nurses should try to understand that academic nurses work very hard to teach students how to be nurses in the best way they know how. They want their new graduates to be ready for the real world, and they greatly appreciate the help that clinical instructors and preceptors provide students and new graduates. Nurse academics do not work 9 to 5; they also work nights and weekends, with the primary goal of forming undergraduate students into nurses and forming graduate students into even *better* nurses. (That being said, it would behoove nurse educators to take note of the perceptions of the nurses surveyed for this book. They describe specific ways in which they could feel better prepared for the real world of nursing.)

Bedside nurses should also realize that nurse researchers strive to make nursing better and to contribute to the betterment of health care for all people. Although their work may sometimes appear to be self-serving, the majority of nurse researchers really do believe their work has value and will make important and lasting contributions to patient care and the lives of nurses in the field. (Unfortunately, they are sometimes so removed from what is happening clinically that how much they actually contribute and advance the profession is questionable.) They also realize that they cannot do their work without the cooperation of other nurses, health care professionals, and patients. The fact is, research is vital and must continue. However, efforts to make it accessible to all nurses must be strengthened.

On the topic of research, it is time it became less intimidating and more integral to the role of nursing. All nurses should receive on-the-job training in various aspects of research, not just minimal training in school programs. The emphasis on evidence-based practice is vital but should not take away from the importance of understanding and being able to critically analyze research. Otherwise, how is the bedside nurse to utilize the research findings to improve practice?

Summary

It is important that the reader understand that what I have said in this chapter is based on my own experience and observations. Not everyone will agree. I have taken this opportunity to express my own concerns about the profession I love in an attempt to make others aware of undercurrents that might otherwise be unknown to them.

As one who has been fortunate enough to straddle the worlds of direct patient care and academia, I can attest to this chasm in nursing. Not only should others acknowledge it, but also efforts must be made to bridge it. Nursing is both a clinical profession and a service one. There is no question that teaching students to become nurses is an honorable and important contribution. But those who teach should be current in their own clinical practice. Taking students to clinical settings is not enough. Researchers who do research on subjects that affect patient care or the work life of nurses are doing vital work, but the work must be relevant, directly applicable, and realistically meaningful. Most of all, efforts must be made to bridge the gap in nursing rather than ignore it.

Chapter 7
Conclusions

The survey responses that provide the foundation for this book validate the current literature but also add to our knowledge about the experience of being a new nurse. In addition, the experiences of new nurses with graduate degrees add a fresh perspective. This chapter highlights some of the more significant issues of concern for recent graduates and offers some recommendations, as outlined in Table 7.1.

Table 7.1: Primary Areas of Concern for Recent Graduates

AREA	ASSOCIATE DEGREE	BACCAL. DEGREE	MASTER'S DEGREE
Time management	X	X	X
Prioritization	X	X	X
Clinical time	X	X	X
Communication with physicians	X	X	
Communication with nurses	X	X	
Communication with staff	X	X	
Communication with other health care disciplines	X	X	
Business practices		X	X
Extensive orientation	X	X	X
Documentation	X	X	
Learning the organization	X	X	X

Getting a Job

Nurse respondents across all educational levels are having trouble finding jobs. Indeed, nurses with master's degrees are concerned that they may have *decreased* their employment opportunities by obtaining a graduate degree. Clearly, something is wrong with this picture.

There are things the profession can do that might enhance the ability of graduates to find jobs:

- Nursing schools must teach marketable skills to new nurses and those nurses graduating with master's degrees. Of course, undergraduates still need clinical experience in the inpatient acute care setting, but perhaps they need less of that and more of other types of nursing experiences. Educators must expose nursing students to all that nurses can do and should encourage nursing students to explore uncharted waters in which nursing expertise can be useful and beneficial. Although undergraduates may think of hospital nursing as traditional and "sexy," faculty can do a lot to enlighten them about myriad other exciting possibilities. As a profession, we need to acknowledge that all clinical experiences are valuable and refrain from conveying to students and new nurses that hospital/acute care experience is the epitome of nursing clinical practice. This may increase their job opportunities, giving everyone more options.

> **NOTE**
>
> *While doing research on nurses with disabilities (Neal-Boylan, 2012), I found that when nurses discover they can no longer work in the hospital, they frequently do not know where else they might find a nursing job. Many subsequently leave nursing.*

- Nursing schools should not accept just anyone into their programs—especially their graduate programs. These schools should require excellent academic preparation, especially solid writing and reading skills. In our effort to respond to intermittent nursing shortages, nursing schools have sometimes admitted students who cannot do the work—and who patients would likely not want to care for them. The fact is, it is unethical to encourage people to become nurses or to obtain graduate nursing degrees if they cannot perform the academic work, they do not see themselves taking care of people (directly or indirectly), or they want to pursue nursing "just to get a job" rather than because they value nursing and what it contributes to society.

In addition, schools must discontinue the practice of nurturing students too much and allowing them to retake tests and repeat classes instead of acknowledging that they are unable to meet high standards. Clearly, these nurses will not be nurtured to such a degree after they graduate; nursing schools do these students a great disservice by sending them off into the real world only to be eaten alive, become discouraged, and potentially leave the profession (or worse, remain as nurses, skewing the public's perception of all nurses by their failure to present a professional appearance, write coherently, or function well in a clinical setting).

NOTE

Telling people who are academically unprepared or incapable that perhaps nursing is not for them is to do these applicants a service. There are many other opportunities for people who want to help others to contribute to society.

- Educators should encourage nurses seeking to obtain a master's degree to learn about the role they would eventually like to have. They should then be required to shadow a nurse in that role, as well as explain what that master's-prepared nurse does and why they want to do it, too. We do a great disservice to master's-degree applicants when we admit them to programs about which they know little, taking their hard-earned money and time, only to send them out into the world where they are not prepared to work in the roles for which employers are hiring. The new graduates may find that they do not like what they are expected to do in these roles and decide to leave the profession.

Clinical Experience

The nurses surveyed were still struggling to transition into the profession and had particular difficulty with clinical decision-making, planning and initiating care, and communicating with physicians. This confirms findings from a study conducted by the National Council of State

Boards of Nursing in 2009 (Hoffart, Waddell, & Young, 2011), and helps illuminate why the Carnegie study (Benner, Sutphen, Leonard, & Day, 2010) recommended increasing clinical experiences, especially outside of acute care, for undergraduate nursing students. The survey respondents perceived this as necessary and vital to being able to make a smooth transition into practice. In fact, the need for more time in clinical and more varied clinical experiences was echoed by all levels of nurses responding to the survey.

Here are a few of the findings from the survey conducted for this book:

- New graduates recognized that for most of them, the days of being able to graduate from nursing school and immediately obtain a job in a hospital are gone—at least for the moment. That means obtaining more clinical time in outpatient settings is particularly critical, both for getting a first job and because there are more patients in the community than in the hospital.

> **NOTE**
>
> *I do not advocate eliminating hospital-based clinical experiences from nursing education. Indeed, as an experienced home health nurse, I have advocated that home and community health nurses need at least 1 year of inpatient experience before they should work in the home setting, because they need to be able to practice autonomously in the home. If a new graduate is unable to get the first year of clinical practice in an acute-care setting, then the community agency should provide an extensive and closely supervised internship before expecting the new nurse to practice autonomously in the home setting.*

- Across the board, nurses who graduated from undergraduate programs not only requested more clinical time for students but also suggested that clinical assignments be more realistic—six to seven patients at a time rather than one or two. These new graduates argued that being able to manage a patient load of one or two patients in no way prepares new nurses to manage a much larger patient load.

- Some respondents recommended front-loading all didactic learning so that students could master the theory behind what they
will need to do in clinical before moving into the clinical setting
to care for patients. Simulation practice could accompany lec-
ture, but actual time in the clinical setting could be postponed to
the end of the semester. This would allow for more concentrated
clinical time.

- Many respondents suggested that there be smaller clinical groups
going to clinical sites while in school. Smaller clinical groups—
particularly for undergraduates—would allow for more one-
on-one time with instructors and with the nurses on the unit.
This is less realistic now than it used to be, however, because it
is becoming increasingly difficult to find clinical placements for
both undergraduate and graduate nursing students.

- New nurse graduates felt that they needed more opportunities to
learn how to use their clinical judgment and make clinical decisions. To aid in this, many schools now use simulation technology to help students learn these important skills. However, not
all schools can afford this technology. Perhaps more case-based
learning would be helpful, so that students must use analytical
skills to make clinical decisions.

- Nurses who had recently graduated from graduate-degree programs also wanted more clinical time, and specified that clinical
experiences should be specific and applicable to the work they
will do. They wanted to learn the clinical skills necessary for
their future jobs and to have more practice making autonomous
decisions.

Communication Skills

New nurses are uncomfortable talking with physicians, their fellow
nurses, and sometimes, professionals from other health care disciplines. It
is becoming increasingly important that nurses know how to collaborate
with other health care professionals. Here are a few suggestions:

- Nursing schools should increase interprofessional opportunities
for students by matching students in clinical experiences and in
simulation practice. Perhaps some classes could mix students
from different health care disciplines to review patient cases and
discuss perspectives on how to approach and manage patients
with different health care needs.

- Interestingly, new graduates do not seem comfortable talking with their fellow nurses, who often prey on anyone new. Role-play can facilitate conversations with these nurses as well as other constituencies, such as physicians and other health care providers. Faculty can simulate these conversations, with or without the use of simulation technology, making sure to convey what the expectations of each group might be. For example, many of the nurse respondents advised nurses coming after them to be humble, ask questions, and not have a chip on their shoulder.

- Nursing education seems to offer insufficient experience talking with families. New graduates feel at a loss as to how to approach families, what to say, and how to establish and maintain rapport. This, too, should be practiced in school. Class time spent learning specific communication skills can help new graduates put their best foot forward in their new job.

Orientation

New graduates from all levels responded to the survey conducted for this book that they should have an in-depth orientation to the new role. It appears that new nurses from undergraduate programs benefit most from lengthy residency programs that provide not only precepted time but also regular classes specifically designed for new graduates, so they can learn how to think and act like nurses and understand the culture of the organization. Here are a few observations on the subject:

- Mentorship is vital. The new graduate should have a mentor and/or preceptor who wants to work with a new graduate and who enjoys teaching and nurturing new professionals. It is important that new graduates have someone with whom they can talk freely and with whom they feel safe to discuss potential mistakes before they make them.

- Nursing schools should incorporate education about how to be a good mentor or preceptor into their leadership classes. Lessons on what to expect from the person you are mentoring or precepting and how best to help that person transition into his or her role help to prepare new graduates if they have to mentor or precept. Such lessons can also help teach them how to work with their own preceptors and mentors to get the most out of these relationships.

- Orientation should be more standardized for new master's-prepared graduates. Some graduates receive no orientation, whereas others have the benefit of participating in residency programs. (These are ideal but rare.) It is unrealistic to expect all private practices or community clinics to give new APRNs extended orientations, but perhaps new graduates could participate in a 6-month extended mentorship with a faculty member when they graduate, giving them someone to talk to and ask questions about their new experiences. This could be a one- to three-credit independent-study program or even be a residency program offered as an option after graduation. New graduates would pay tuition for the privilege but would benefit greatly from structured time with faculty. The faculty member could also make site visits as part of this class to observe the new graduate and make suggestions. This would be different from the precepted experiences and site visits made while students are in school, because the new graduates would now be legally responsible for their decisions.

NOTE

This model could also be applied to graduates from non-APRN programs. New graduates could be assigned a faculty mentor after graduation if they do not have a mentor in their new practice setting.

Behavior

New graduates generally do not know how to behave once they are on their own in the clinical setting. This is aside from how they care for patients and instead refers to how they manage their time, interact with others, learn the organization, and determine their boundaries. Here are a few of the major concerns:

- New nurse graduates need more work learning how to multitask, prioritize, and delegate. This problem may become less prevalent if nursing schools require students to care for six or seven patients at a time while in school, instead of one or two. It is difficult to learn how to manage your time and prioritize if you are not put in a position that requires you to do more than one important thing at a time. Role-play can be a helpful tool for teaching students how to delegate work to staff, technicians, and aides.

> **NOTE**
>
> *Back when I was a brand-new graduate, I told a nurse's aide that she was late providing a.m. (morning) care to the patient. No sooner were the words out of my mouth than my preceptor pulled me by the ear into the break room to explain that while I was the RN, I had no business talking to the aide that way. I learned that there are ways of delegating work, that there are ways of learning whether others are actually slacking or have in fact prioritized their patient load, and how to show appreciation for the work others do to lighten my load. These lessons can be taught only through practice and role-modeling.*

- Nurses who responded to the survey conducted for this book noted that they did not feel they knew their boundaries. By this, they meant many different things, including communication with others, what to report as noteworthy, and the chain of command in the nursing hierarchy as well as in the organization's hierarchy. Although every organization is different, some basic rules apply, and it would be helpful to instruct students about how to manage complex nonclinical situations. It's almost as important to know how to function in the health care environment with regard to the day-to-day expectations as it is to be able to perform clinical skills.

> **NOTE**
>
> *In my research with home health nurses (Neal-Boylan, 2009), I found it takes a good 2 years working in the home setting for a nurse to become truly autonomous, regardless of previous work settings. Much of this has to do with learning how to work in an unstructured setting, dealing with paperwork, and managing reimbursement rather than the actual clinical skills involved in caring for patients. This is surely as true in other nursing settings.*

- As a profession, we should try to move away from the idea of "nurse heroics" (Neal-Boylan, 2012)—that we do not need to rest, eat, sleep, or enjoy life because our patients come first. Of course, our patients *do* come first, but burnout is a serious issue in nursing and contributes to the loss of nurses from the profession. We can care for our patients without becoming alienated from our peers if we take our scheduled breaks and vacation time.

Paperwork

Students are not always exposed to the paperwork that is required outside of direct patient care. They typically learn how to document the care they provide, but they may not learn all the other administrative minutia that goes into making the organization work. Increasing students' awareness of the existence of other types of administrative responsibilities may help make this seem less daunting when they graduate. Also, requiring them to do all the paperwork that a nurse on a unit or in an agency must do in a given day will help prepare them for the real world. As much as we may not like it, the paperwork—regardless of setting—is a required part of nursing work.

NOTE

Despite the increasing use of electronic health records, nurses still use the term "paperwork" to refer to all of the administrative aspects of nursing.

To the New Nurse Graduate

It is important for new graduates to recognize that nurse educators work very hard to design and revise curricula to meet the needs of their students. Nursing schools must be accredited—a process that is lengthy and revealing, uncovering all the areas in which a program is strong, as well as all the areas in which it is deficient. Between accreditation reviews, nursing schools spend a great deal of time trying to determine what works and what does not work. Curriculum is a topic of endless meetings and discussion, and its review and revision are dynamic processes. Schools use feedback from their current students, alumni, clinical partners, faculty, and others to keep curricula as vital and practical as possible. Students and graduates can help their alma maters by responding to surveys sent by their schools and by keeping in touch with faculty. Feedback about how the curriculum relates to current nursing practice and needs within the health care environment is vital to making sure that nursing schools serve the needs of their students and graduates.

All that being said, regardless of whether they graduate with an associate's degree or baccalaureate degree in nursing, new undergraduate-prepared nurses have a lot with which to contend: simply finding a job, finding a job they *like*, becoming integrated into the profession and in the organization, and more. There is always going to be some culture shock and a learning curve. That is to be expected. To help with that learning curve, new nurses would do well to review and be mindful of the advice given by survey respondents in this book:

- **Be humble.** Although you have learned a lot, you are a novice nurse and should display a willingness and openness to learn from more experienced nurses.

- **Show respect.** It is critical to show respect for experienced nurses and what they know.

- **Ask questions, listen carefully to the answers, and remember them.** Try not to be a person who has to be told the same thing more than once. Make notes, and go back to your books and resources when you encounter something new.

- **Know your resources.** You will not always know the answer or what to do next, regardless of how well-educated you are or how long you have been a nurse. That is alright. Once you think you know everything, you have stopped being a lifelong learner. Find books you can trust. Read the journals and make it a priority to keep current. Know where you can find the information you need, and keep it at your fingertips. This is easier now more than ever with current technology.

- **Do your homework, even though you are no longer in school.** Good nurses are lifelong learners regardless of how many letters they have after their names or how many degrees or certificates they have earned.

- **Don't ever, ever fake it.** Lives might be at risk. It is better to appear ignorant than to pretend you know something you do not and potentially harm a patient or put your colleagues in a bad position. People will have more respect for you if you admit what you do not know than if you pretend you do know. However, if you do your homework and look up things you do not know, then you will be prepared to ask intelligent questions.

- **Don't be afraid to talk to physicians.** Yes, they can be intimidating. But newer physicians are receiving more and more training in working with other disciplines and in presenting a softer side than the all-knowing "G-d" of medicine. In a practical sense, medical residents learn much of what they ultimately know from nurses. There should be mutual respect for each of our professions—although this is an evolving movement.

- **Network and find a solid support system.** Know from whom you can seek advice and feel comfortable revealing your ignorance. Seek and obtain comfort and solace from your family and friends on a regular basis. Find peers and colleagues with whom you can ventilate your concerns and share your nursing joys and sorrows. These can become lifelong friendships.

- **Take care of yourself.** Do not feel guilty when you use your vacation days or call out sick when you are sick. We often lie awake thinking of our patients, but make sure you have fun and time to regenerate, or you will do your patients no good the next time you care for them.

- **When you are ready, mentor others.** Do not be a nurse who eats your young. Try very hard not to perpetuate this adage. Remember how you feel *now* as a new graduate, and use the memory to help make you more empathetic with other new graduates as you mature in your role. Being hard on new graduates or nurses new to a role or setting does not make you appear better than they are; it only diminishes you in their eyes and hurts the profession. Do not spoon-feed new nurses, but make them feel welcome into our world and happy to be among us.

To the New Master's-Prepared Graduate

This book attempted to capture the perspectives of recent master's-prepared graduates. More of this information could be helpful to inform graduate curricula. What follows are some observations and recommendations based on the survey responses and my own experience.

- **Research.** It is important for someone going into or contemplating entering a graduate program to do some research into the various types of roles available and identify why they are pursuing a particular role or position. This is likely to prevent heartache later, when the new graduate has trouble finding a job or does not like the job he or she found.

- **Continue your education.** For those who have already graduated, it might be necessary to go back to school for a post master's certificate to enhance employment opportunities. Short of that, getting a clinical certificate in a specialty might be helpful, although these often require a certain number of clinical hours in the specialty before one can sit for the exam. The certificate might be in nursing or outside of nursing. For example, I took an online module program over the course of a year to obtain a certificate in rheumatology from the American College of Rheumatology. This helped when I applied for a job in an internal medicine practice that preferred that each of its providers have a "specialty" area in addition to internal medicine.

- **Attend conferences.** This can educate or update you in areas in which you feel deficient. In addition to being required for recertification in many states, continuing education credits also look good on a résumé.

- **Joining nursing organizations.** Joining certain nursing organizations might add caché to your résumé when you apply for a job. Actively participate in the organization, and do what you can to advance the profession.

- **Maintain a relationship with a favorite faculty member.** Ideally, ask this person to mentor you at least through your first year—if not longer post graduation. It will help to have someone who views you as a colleague with whom to discuss your new experiences. If you plan to do research or write for publication (which you should), it will help you to be associated with someone who has a track record in these areas and can help to make your name known.

Summary

I hope this book has provided valuable insights for current students, recent graduates, nurse educators, and nurse administrators in clinical settings. Although much of the information in this book is not new, it confirms what the literature has discussed with regard to undergraduates and sheds light on the perspectives of nurses with new graduate degrees—although much more work needs to be done to explore the perceptions of new graduates, especially those with graduate degrees. It would be particularly interesting to see how new graduates of DNP programs view their academic preparation.

Although this book was based mostly on the responses to a survey conducted among new nurse graduates, I have injected my own opinions and biases, gleaned from being a nurse for more than 30 years and having worked in many different types of clinical and academic settings. My opinion—which may disturb some people—should not necessarily count more than anyone else's, but it should count for something, as I have conducted a successful academic career while always maintaining a clinical practice and raising a family. Some may say that I am not worthy, because I do not have six-figure grants in my portfolio. My counterargument is that the small private grants I have been awarded have allowed me to conduct research that has had direct meaning for and application to nurses and patients. I take some satisfaction in that.

I encourage others to brave potential criticism from their nurse colleagues to vent their concerns about what is happening in the profession. Nurses, above all, are great listeners, and we do want the best for the profession and our patients. Even if others do not agree, you will be heard—and perhaps what you have to say will spur change.

Nursing has a long and wonderful history. Hopefully, we also have a bright future that will show meaningful change but also retain what those of us who have stayed the course still love most about the profession. I hope you love it—or come to love it—as much as I do.

References

Aiken, L., Clarke, S., Cheung, R., Sloane, D., & Silber, J. (2003). Educational levels of hospital nurses and surgical patient mortality. *Journal of the American Medical Association, 290*(12), 1617–1623.

Allen, L. (2008). The nursing shortage continues as faculty shortage grows. *Nursing Economics, 26*(1), 35–40.

American Association of Colleges of Nursing (AACN). (2011). Nursing fact sheet. Retrieved from http://www.aacn.nche.edu/media-relations/fact-sheets/nursing-fact-sheet

American Association of Colleges of Nursing (AACN). (2011). *The essentials of master's education in nursing.* Washington, DC: Author. Retrieved from http://www.aacn.nche.edu/education-resources/MastersEssentials11.pdf

American Nurses Association (ANA). (1965). Education for nursing. *American Journal of Nursing, 65*(12), 106–111.

Benner, P. (1984). *From novice to expert: Excellence and power in clinical nursing practice.* Menlo Park, CA: Addison-Wesley.

Benner, P., Sutphen, M., Leonard, V., & Day, L. (2010). *Educating nurses: A call for radical transformation.* San Francisco: Jossey-Bass.

Black, L., Spetz, J., & Harrington, C. (2008). Nurses working outside of nursing: Societal trend or workplace crisis? *Policy, Politics & Nursing Practice, 9*(3), 143—157.

Black, L., Spetz, J., & Harrington, C. (2010). Nurses who do not nurse: Factors that predict non-nursing work in the U.S. registered nursing labor market. *Nursing Economics, 28*(4), 245—254.

Blanzola, C., Lindeman, R., & King, M. L. (2004). Nurse internship pathway to clinical comfort, confidence, and competency. *Journal for Nurses in Staff Development, 20,* 27–37.

Brooks, K., & Shepherd, J. M. (1992). Professionalism versus general critical thinking abilities of senior nursing students in four types of nursing curricula. *Journal of Professional Nursing, 8*(2), 87–95.

Casey, K., Fink, R., Krugman, M., & Probst, J. (2004). The graduate nurse experience. *Journal of Nursing Administration, 34*(6), 303–311.

Cruikshank, B. M., & Lakin, J. A. (1986). Professional and employment characteristics of NPs with master's and non-master's preparation. *Nurse Practitioner, 11*(11), 45–52.

Donner, G. J., & Waddell, J. (2011). Are we paying enough attention to clarifying our vision for master's-prepared nurses and ensuring that educational programs and workplaces are prepared to help achieve that vision? An invitation to engage in an important conversation. *Canadian Journal of Nursing Leadership, 24*(2), 26–30, 31–35.

Dracup, K. (2012). *Master's nursing programs.* Retrieved from http://www.aacn.nche.edu/education-resources/msn-article

Drennan, J. (2008). Professional and academic destination of master's in nursing graduates: A national survey. *Nurse Education Today, 28,* 751–759.

Drennan, J., & Hyde, A. (2008). Social selection and professional regulation for master's degrees for nurses. *Journal of Advanced Nursing, 63*(5), 486–493.

Feldman, A. (2008). Does academic culture support translational research? *CTS: Clinical and Translational Science, 1*(2), 87–88.

Glazer, J. (1988). The master's degree. Washington, DC: ERIC Digest. ERIC Clearing House on Higher Education.

Goode, C. J., Pinkerton, S., McCausland, M., Southard, P., Graham, R., & Kresk, C. (2001). Documenting chief nursing officers' preference for BSN-prepared nurses. *Journal of Nursing Administration, 31*(2), 55–59.

Health Resources and Services Administration. (2008). *The registered nurse population: Initial findings from the 2008 National Sample Survey of Registered Nurses.* Retrieved from http://bhpr.hrsa.gov/healthworkforce/rnsurveys/rnsurveyinitial2008.pdf

Health Resources and Services Administration. (2010, September). *The registered nurse population: Findings from the 2008 National Sample Survey of Registered Nurses.* Washington, DC: U.S. Department of Health and Human Services.

Hoffart, N., Waddell, A., & Young, M. B. (2011). A model of new nurse transition. *Journal of Professional Nursing, 27*(6), 334–343.

Institute of Medicine of the National Academies. (2010). *The future of nursing: Leading change, advancing health.* Washington, DC: The National Academies Press.

Jacobs, L., DiMattio, M., Bishop, T., & Fields, S. (1998). The baccalaureate degree in nursing as an entry-level requirement for professional nursing practice. *Journal of Professional Nursing, 14*(4), 225–233.

Kalman, M., Wells, M., & Gavan, G. S. (2009). Returning to school: Experiences of female baccalaureate registered nurse students. *Journal of the New York State Nurses Association,* 11–16.

Katz, P. (2005). *Retrieving the master's degree from the dustbin of history: A report for the members of the American Historical Association.* Washington, DC: American Historical Association.

Kramer, M. (1974). *Reality shock: Why nurses leave nursing.* St. Louis: Mosby.

Lawler, T., & Rose, M. (1987). Professionalization: A comparison among generic baccalaureate, ADN and RN/BSN nurses. *Nurse Educator, 12*(3), 19–22.

Martin, K., & Wilson, C. B. (2011). Newly registered nurses' experience in the first year of practice: A phenomenological study. *International Journal of Human Caring, 15*(2), 21–30.

McIntosh, B., Rambur, B., Palumbo, M. V., & Mongeon, J. (2003). The older nurse: Clues for retention. *Nurse and Health Policy Review, 2,* 61–77.

McKenna, B. G., Smith, N. A., Poole, S. J., & Coverdale, J. H. (2003). Horizontal violence: Experiences of registered nurses in their first year of practice. *Journal of Advanced Nursing, 42*(1), 90–96.

Morgan, J. C., & Lynn, M. R. (2009). Satisfaction in the context of the shortage. *Journal of Nursing Management, 17*(3), 401–410.

National Council of State Boards of Nursing (NCSBN). (2009). *Report of findings from the post-entry competence study. Research brief, Vol. 38.* Chicago: Author. Retrieved from https://www.ncsbn.org/09_PostEntryCompetenceStudy_Vol38_WEB_final_081909.pdf

National League for Nursing. (1977). Criteria for the appraisal of baccalaureate and higher degree programs in nursing. New York, NY: Author.

National League for Nursing. (2010, June 29). Master's education is focus of NLN *Reflection & Dialogue. Retrieved from* http://www.nln.org/newsreleases/masters_r&d_062910.htm

Neal-Boylan, L. J. (2009). *On becoming a home health nurse: Practice meets theory in home care nursing* (2nd ed.). National Association for Home Care.

Neal-Boylan, L. (2012). *Registered nurses with disabilities: Professional issues and job retention.* New York: Springer.

Nelson, M. (2002, May 31). Education for professional nursing practice: Looking backward into the future. *Online Journal of Issues in Nursing,* (7)2. Retrieved from www.nursingworld.org/MainMenuCategories/ANAMarketplace/ANAPeriodicals/OJIN/TableofContents/Volume72002/No2May2002/EducationforProfessionalNursingPractice.aspx

Newman, M. A. (2008). *Transforming presence: The difference that nursing makes.* Philadelphia: F. A. Davis.

Nightingale, F. (1860). *Notes on nursing: What it is and what it is not.* Retrieved from http://digital.library.upenn.edu/women/nightingale/nursing/nursing.html#III

Orsolini-Hain, L. (2012). The Institute of Medicine's future of nursing report: What are the implications for associate degree nursing education? *Teaching and Learning in Nursing, 7,* 74–77.

Orsolini-Hain, L., & Waters, V. (2009). Education evolution: A historical perspective of associate degree nursing. *Journal of Nursing Education, 48*(5), 266–271. doi: 10.9999/01484834-20090416-05

Pardue, S. F. (1987). Decision-making skills and critical thinking ability among associate degree, diploma, baccalaureate, and master's-prepared nurses. *Journal of Nursing Education, 26*(9), 354–361.

Radzyminaki, S. (2005). Advances in graduate nursing education: Beyond the advanced practice nurse. *Journal of Professional Nursing, 21*(2), 110–125.

Rambur, B., McIntosh, B., Palumbo, M. V., & Reinier, K. (2005). Education as a determinant of career retention and job satisfaction among registered nurses. *Journal of Nursing Scholarship, 37*(2), 185–192.

Sexton, K. A., Hunt, C. E., Cox, K. S., Teasley, S. L., & Carroll, C. A. (2008). Differentiating the workplace needs of nurses by academic preparation and years in nursing. *Journal of Professional Nursing, 24*, 105–108.

Spurr, S. H. (1970). *Academic degree structures: innovative approaches.* New York: McGraw-Hill.

Stevenson, E. L., (2003). Future trends in nursing employment: The nursing shortage has made choosing the right career path easier. *AJN, 103* (career guide suppl), 19–25.

Sullivan, G. C., Anderson, D. L., & Houde, S. C. (1983). The master's degree in nursing: Controversy in nomenclature. *Journal of Nursing Education, 22*(8), 344–347.

Thomas, S. P. (2003). Anger: the mismanaged emotion. *MEDSURG Nursing, 12*, 103–110.

Ulrich, B., Krozek, C., Early, S., Ashlock, C. H., Africa, L. M., & Carman, M. L. (2010). Improving retention, confidence, and competence of new graduate nurses: Results from a 10-year longitudinal database. *Nursing Economic$, 28*(6), 363–375.

Valiga, T. M. (2002). The nursing faculty shortage. NLN perspective presentation to the National Advisory Council on Nurse Education and Practice (NACNEP). Retrieved from http://www.nln.org/Research/facultyshortage.htm

Warren, J. I., & Mills, M. E. (2009). Motivating registered nurses to return for an advanced degree. *The Journal of Continuing Education in Nursing, 40*(5), 200–207.

Watson-Gegeo, K. A. (2005). Teaching to transform and the dark side of "being professional." *ReVision, 28*(2), 43–48.

Wieland, D., Altmiller, G. M., Dorr, M. T., & Wolf, Z. R. (2007). Clinical transition of baccalaureate nursing students during preceptored, pregraduation practicums. *Nursing Education Perspectives, 28,* 315–321.

Wolff, A. C., Pesut, B., & Regan, S. (2009). New graduate nurse practice readiness: Perspectives on the context shaping our understanding and expectations. *Nurse Education Today, 30,* 187–191.

Wood, D. (2009). Why have nurses left the profession? *NurseZone.* Retrieved from http://www.nursezone.com/nursing-news-events/more-news/Why-Have-Nurses-Left-the-Profession_29118.aspx

Index